Frontispiece. "Study of Frost by Daggy," oil on canvas (inscribed "Jan. 20th, 1884"). This portrait by Augustus S. Daggy, one of Frost's closest friends, was painted shortly after the period when the two were fellow students in a class conducted by Thomas Eakins at the Pennsylvania Academy of Fine Arts.

Study of Frost –   by Dacey
                                                         Jan - 20th
                                                            1884

The
A. B. FROST
BOOK

by Henry M. Reed

With a foreword by Eugene V. Connett

CHARLES E. TUTTLE COMPANY

Rutland   *Vermont*

Representatives
Continental Europe: BOXERBOOKS, INC., *Zurich*
British Isles: PRENTICE-HALL INTERNATIONAL, INC., *London*
Australasia: PAUL FLESCH & CO., PTY. LTD., *Melbourne*
Canada: m. g. hurtig ltd., *Edmonton*

Published by the Charles E. Tuttle Company, Inc.
of Rutland, Vermont & Tokyo, Japan
with editorial offices at
Suido 1-chome, 2-6, Bunkyo-ku, Tokyo

Copyright in Japan, 1967
by Charles E. Tuttle Co.

Library of Congress Catalog Card No. 67-21929

First printing, 1967

Book design & typography by Florence Sakade
Layout of plates by Shigeo Katakura

PRINTED IN JAPAN

❆ *Table of Contents* ❆

❊ *List of Illustrations* ❊

⁂ *Foreword* ⁂

by Eugene V. Connett

B. FROST was the "Sportsman's Artist." No one ever equaled his ability to depict the mood, the detail, the authenticity of sporting scenes. This was and is the secret of the intense pleasure a sportsman feels as he drinks in the scene of a Frost shooting painting or drawing. In the thirty-seven years during which I edited and published sporting books and prints, I have seen and studied hundreds of specimens of sporting art. My approach to this work was always a careful look for discrepancies and errors. My approach to studying a picture by Frost was just the opposite—a confident expectation to revel in the enjoyment of all that makes shooting the passionate pleasure it is to me.

Many readers of this book will wonder—just as I did when I first read the manuscript—who is Henry Reed, and what does he know about Frost? Take a good look at the dozens of Frost pictures in this book and then realize that with very few exceptions, all these are in Mr. Reed's own collection. Then you should know that he has been in touch with every member of the Frost family who could contribute any facts about the artist, and he has studied many original letters, etc., that had information to yield. There is no doubt in my mind that Henry

Reed is the outstanding authority on the work and life of A. B. Frost. How fortunate we are that he has put his knowledge in such a beautiful book!

When I saw the first draft of this book, I recall feeling happy that another volume about A. B. Frost was to be written. The book I had published in 1933, written by Henry W. Lanier, had always been a disappointment to me.

When I saw the final draft of Mr. Reed's manuscript, I was, very frankly, surprised and delighted. It had turned out so much better than I had expected it would! I heartily congratulate the author and the publisher for producing such a splendid appreciation for and monument to the memory of a great artist and his talented family.

Like all sportsmen of my era, I was brought up on Frost's shooting prints, as well as books full of his illustrations. At one time my father lived in Convent Station, not far from "Moneysunk," the Frost home. Dad used to play golf with Mr. Frost. I regret to say I never met him, as I was away at college, etc., most of the time. However, my father, who was no mean practitioner of the art, often said that Mr. Frost on the golf course raised the art of cursing to sublime levels.

John Frost was later a close friend of mine. In fact, it was because of my insistent nagging that John finally consented to paint sporting pictures. He had always refused to do it as he didn't want to appear to be leaning on his father's reputation. After I got him started on that series for *The Sportsman* magazine, he actually seemed enthusiastic about it. Jack loved fishing and shooting, and painting such subjects came very naturally to him. I shall never forgive myself for not preserving more carefully all the little pencil sketches on his letters. He certainly had his father's ability to draw delightful, witty little caricatures.

It would have been natural for Henry Reed to have lifted much of the material from the Lanier book, but he didn't. He struck out on his own, did an enormous amount of original research, and has written a completely new and infinitely superior book. The American public, or at least that part of it interested in art and sport, owes Mr. Reed an enthusiastic vote of thanks.

As a publisher of fine sporting books for many years, I can say without fear of contradiction, that the Charles E. Tuttle Company, Inc., also deserves the thanks of present and future generations for having the courage to make the great investment required in reproducing so many Frost pictures in color and thus preserving them for all time.

I am supposed to be writing a short foreword to this book—not a sales blurb. But I simply can't refrain from urging everyone interested in American art and sport to put this book in his library, so his children and his grandchildren may know about this distinguished illustrator and painter and his greatly talented family.

❈ *Acknowledgments* ❈

FIRST OF ALL *I must thank the living relatives of A. B. Frost, particularly Mr. Francis Macdonald and the artist's grandchildren, Priscilla Frost Milliman and John Frost, Jr., for allowing me to undertake this project and for giving me so completely their trust and confidence.*

Special thanks also are to be given to the family of Augustus S. Daggy, the artist's best friend, for the use of letters and other material so vital in the preparation of this work.

I wish also to thank Robert M. Lunny, director, and his staff of the New Jersey Historical Society; Dr. Kenneth Prescott, director, and Mrs. Leah Sloshberg, curator, and their staff at the New Jersey State Museum; William C. Agee, associate curator of the Whitney Museum of American Art; William H. McCarthy and Clive Driver of the Philip H. and A. S. W. Rosenbach Foundation; Miss Ellen Shaffer and her staff of the Rare Book Department of the Philadelphia Free Public Library; the Joel Chandler Harris Estate; and the Emory University Library for their technical assistance and use of their materials.

To Ernest Hickok and Charles Borst may I express my appreciation for encouraging me to undertake this project and to John Nighland and Montagu Hankin for finding me my first sporting prints by Frost and consequently getting me started on such an adventure.

Finally may I give a special expression of appreciation to Eugene V. Connett for putting his very distinguished name alongside my very obscure one in writing such a warm introduction to this volume.

HENRY M. REED

Caldwell, New Jersey

The Artist

Who Let One Half of the Country Know
How the Other Half Lived

WERE A. B. FROST known to us today as simply the dean of American illustrators as well as America's outstanding sporting artist, a definitive treatise on his life and work would be a worthwhile project on these attributes alone. When we add to these basic qualities his skill as a fine painter and his irresistible style as an author and humorist, we find in A. B. Frost the outstanding chronicler of a broad segment of a vanished era.

While Frederic Remington and Charles M. Russell and so many others depicted that great period in our history involving the West—our frontiers and vanishing Indian civilization—A. B. Frost was pictorially writing the chapter involving the Eastern scene: the farmers, barnyards, plantation life, the creatures and birds of the marshes and uplands, and the men who hunted them.

Following Frost's death in 1928, the *Philadelphia Public Ledger*, describing him as "the most American of American artists" said:

A generation that finds enjoyment in the slinky horrors of contemporary illustration or that sees something significant in the sketchy, grotesque, and sometimes extremely bewildering work of artists who "go modern" because they can not learn to draw would view Mr. Frost's work as somehow meaningless. Yet it was Frost who, by his great skill, talent, and patience, actually let one-half of the country know how the other half lived. The people he drew were real people. His animals were the very creatures of barnyards and meadows. No other artist was ever able to make a sky seem so clear or a reach of open natural land so true to reality. Frost was a great draughtsman, who preferred truth to fads. Few of his sort remain.

A. B. Frost was the primary illustrator of more than 90 published books. Among the most notable of the many authors whose works he illustrated, we find such distinguished names as Lewis Carroll, Charles Dickens, Joel Chandler Harris, Mark Twain, Theodore Roosevelt, Frank Stockton, William Thackeray, and many others. For nearly 50 continuous years his illustrations appeared in the leading magazines including *Harper's*, *Scribner's*, *Collier's*, *Century*, *Puck*, and *Life*. His own books—*Stuff & Nonsense*, *The Bull Calf and Other Tales*, and *Carlo*—were recognized as masterpieces of comedy.

The *New York World*, in an editorial obituary, wrote:

> A capital draftsman, racy of the soil as Mark Twain or Uncle Remus (both of whom he illustrated), unembittered, gusty as an Elizabethan, Frost will remain as one of the best America has produced. To pass from the shoddiness of the present-day "comic" to Frost's work is like coming out of a cheap cabaret into a delightful performance of Gilbert and Sullivan.

It would be an unfortunate miscalculation, however, to regard Frost's artistic talent solely in terms of "illustrator" or comic "caricaturist." His serious art, although less known, was strongly influenced by his distinguished teachers Thomas Eakins and William Merritt Chase. Said *Metropolitan* magazine in April, 1905:

> As a painter in oils, Mr. Frost has exhibited both here and abroad. His contributions in this medium to the Paris Exposition in 1900 won for him the unstinted praise of the most exacting critics of the French Capital.

An attempt to single out any one or group of Frost's prodigious lifelong output as his most noteworthy work would be almost impossible; however, the "Shooting Pictures" portfolio, published by Charles Scribner's Sons in 1895 and the unforgettable Brer Rabbit from *Uncle Remus* would have to be near the top of such a list.

The "Shooting Pictures" portfolio, which will be dealt with at some length later in this volume, is a set of 12 lithographs of various hunting scenes. These prints are the most eagerly sought Frost collector's items and are very difficult to find. Lucky indeed is the collector-sportsman whose walls are adorned by these colorful and exciting portrayals of his favorite pastime, for Frost has captured the very tense instant when the quail is about to flush under the cold moist nose of the quivering pointer, or the ducks are suspiciously circling, getting ready to stool over the decoys of the nervous hunter, whose heart is pounding as he crouches low in his blind.

Theodore Roosevelt, great sportsman and outdoorsman during the 1880's and 90's prior to becoming our nation's President, wrote to Frost in 1885:

DEAR MR. FROST:

In the words of the immortal bard of Avon, damn the expense! I want at least *five* pictures; and six if you can give them.

I think it will be an immense improvement to have the bear in the foreground; if not too much trouble have the figures portraits—myself giving the shot, and my companion whose photograph you have kneeling beside me. (It is the photograph of the man kneeling with a

§2. Arthur Burdett Frost in his studio (*c.* 1904). The painting on the easel is "The Horrid Thing."

§3. "The Monroe Doctrine," gouache (1904). One of the artist's best-known and beloved genre works, this painting was reproduced originally in *A Book of Drawings* written by Frost.

§4. RIGHT: "The Candlestick Girl," water color (1883). The model in this painting is thought to be Miss Emily Phillips who shortly after this painting was completed became Mrs. A. B. Frost.

§5. "An Autumn Landscape," oil on canvas (1900).

fur cap; he has a dark moustache). Don't bother yourself about either; the cowboy's portrait is unimportant.

The mountain ram picture was first rate; the Bad Lands have just the eccentric character you gave them; indeed the likeness was wonderful. Don't tone it down too much; the rocks ought to look queer and bizarre.

Most truly yours,
THEODORE ROOSEVELT

Just what is there about Frost's art that attracted so much attention back in 1874, when his first illustrations were published, and which has continued down through the years during which time his drawings have illustrated some of the classics in American literature?

Why is it in the present day that we are witnessing a new rush and scramble by Frost collectors to possess any example of his work?

Frank Stockton referred to Frost as "the most American of American artists." Frost was completely honest in his work, his characters are absolutely real "everyday folk" without glamor or pretense, and yet these attributes alone are far from sufficient prerequisites for recognition. Frost's characters have that quaint indescribable quality—you get the feeling in his pictures that something is on the verge of erupting as he captures that electric instant of suspense just before the explosion. And the articulation of the body! He could draw a man with his back to the observer, dressed in a sack suit and you can practically see the expression on the subject's face! Whether it was complete relaxation or quivering tension, he captured it with just a few strokes from his sure, swift fingers. There is one scene in particular—an oil painting on canvas measuring only 10″ by 17″—entitled an "Outdoor Sacrament" and depicting a prayer meeting involving more than 60 figures sitting, kneeling, or standing in various prayerful meditative positions. The artist captures completely the solemn reverence of the occasion, including the impending downpour from heavy, rain-filled clouds rolling down over the majestic mountains with trees forming an aesthetic background. And yet during the same time in his career came his unforgettable pictorial story of the cat who ate rat poison, scenes from which are such wild, hilarious episodes that the whole story leaves the viewer weak and breathless from laughter. His sketchbooks are replete with pencil caricatures of human forms in various poses, reclining, sitting, standing, talking, screaming, but almost always on the verge of violent action. There is a study of a shabbily dressed man, hand clutched to his throat with a wild look in his eye, who seems limply suspended like a puppet on a string, staggering, reeling, and flopping about in the most realistic manner. And dogs—he loved dogs—he left page after page of dog studies; hunting dogs pointing, of course, plus pencil sketches of dogs sleeping, curled up, stretched out. It is said that whenever Frost went to the home of a friend who owned a dog, he immediately asked for a sheet of paper and dashed off a little gem which he invariably signed and handed to the dog's master.

[23]

In Joel Chandler Harris' immortal "Uncle Remus" series, A. B. Frost truly earned his reputation as a master draftsman and his drawings helped establish Brer Rabbit as one of the classic characters in American literature. In the introduction to his book, *Uncle Remus, His Songs and His Sayings,* Harris credits his illustrator with much of the success of this edition of his book in the following excerpt from his open letter of introduction:

Because you have taken it under your hand and made it yours. Because you have breathed the breath of life into these amiable brethren of wood and field. Because by a stroke here and a touch there, you have conveyed into their quaint antics the illumination of your own inimitable humor, which is as true to our sun and soil as it is to the spirit and essence of the matter set forth. The book was mine, but now you have made it yours, both sap and pith.

Success Comes Early

NICHOLAS FROST brought the family name to America and Eliot, Maine, around 1634, although he had made a brief visit to Boston a few years before. His son, Major Charles Frost, at one time military governor of Maine, was killed in an Indian ambush on his way to church on the fourth of July, 1697, an occasion commemorated in 1897 by the Eliot Historical Society.

A. B. Frost's father, Prof. John Frost, was born in Kennebunk, Maine, Jan. 26, 1800. He graduated from Harvard in 1822. The following year he became headmaster of the Mayhew School in Boston, until 1827 when he moved to Philadelphia. In 1838 he was appointed professor of belles lettres in the Central High School in Philadelphia. He received an LL.D. degree from Franklin and Marshall College in 1843. Beginning in 1845 he devoted his time exclusively to histories and biographies, of which, with the assistance of a staff of writers, he had over 300 published, including many important histories.

On May 4, 1830, he married Sarah Ann Burdett in a ceremony conducted by Ralph Waldo Emerson, minister of the Second Church (Unitarian) in Boston and better remembered today as a famous American poet.

Prof. Frost died on December 28, 1859, leaving his large family a fine reputation, although little money.

One of the most important bearers of the Frost name in this long and distinguished list of Americans is the late renowned poet, Robert Frost, a distant cousin of A. B. Frost.

Arthur Burdett Frost, born January 17, 1851, was one of ten children; however, only two survived beyond the artist's teenage years. His sister, Sarah Annie Frost, became an authoress. Her most notable work, *Almost a Man* [American Tract Society, New York, 1877], was illustrated by her brother Arthur. Frost's brother, Charles, became the owner of *Godey's Ladies Book*, in which his father had had an interest, and authored a few books of his own under the pseudonym of C. S. Ribbler. He also wrote the jingles for his brother Arthur's first book, *Stuff & Nonsense*, and had originated a perpetual calendar, as well as Frost's Comprehensive Calendar, which is still being published.

In 1874 Arthur Burdett Frost was just a struggling young lithographer, and not a very good one either, when Dame Fortune struck like a bolt of lightning and catapulted the 23-year-old Frost into immediate fame and prominence. It happened this way:

Charles Heber Clarke, humorist and author (writing under the pseudonym of Max Adeler), was completing the manuscript for his new book *Out of the Hurly Burly* when his brother William J. Clarke, a friend of Frost, suggested that Arthur might have talent enough to do a few sketches for the book. A few sketches indeed! The book came out with nearly 400 illustrations, almost all of them by young Arthur Frost.

The book was an immediate sensation and went on to sell over a million copies including translations into foreign languages. The author, even before publication, must have had some premonition of success for both his book and the career of his youthful illustrator when he made the following remarks in the book's preface:

> If this little venture shall achieve popularity, I must attribute the fact largely to the admirable pictures with which it has been adorned by the artists whose names appear upon the title-page. I wish to direct attention especially to the humorous pictures of Mr. Arthur B. Frost. This artist makes his first appearance before the public in these pages. These are the only drawings upon wood he has ever executed, and they are so nicely illustrative of the text, they display so much originality and versatility, and they have such genial humor, with so little extravagance and exaggeration, that they seem to me surely to give promise of a prosperous career for the artist.

The author's prefatory remarks were understatements compared to the opinions of the press which later appeared. Said the *Philadelphia Evening Bulletin:*

> The illustrations are much the best that have ever been given in any American book of humor. There are nearly four hundred of them, most of which were designed by Mr. Arthur B. Frost, a young man whose genius has had its first good chance in this work, and who is sure to become famous as a designer, especially in the line of the grotesque and comical.

The *Wilmington Commercial* said:

> The illustrations are profuse, and they are, nevertheless, excellent in design and execution. Most of them are by Mr. A. B. Frost, whose success is such as to put him at once in the foremost rank of American humorous artists. They really illustrate the text, and add in an important degree to its sum-total of genial pleasantry.

From the *Philadelphia Item:*

> We have not laughed so much in a year. Pure fun, lots of fun, greet you on every page, and more amusement and entertainment can be found in this one volume than any other half-dozen comical books we have read this season. It contains 400 of the best American illustrations we have ever seen.

Frost hardly had time to bask in the warmth of his new-found fame and notoriety, for he was such a shy and retiring individual, never completely satisfied with his work, that celebration or exuberance was completely inconsistent with his personality. Instead he immediately plunged into his career of nearly 50 years of continuous hard work and prolific output of drawings, paintings, sketches, and illustrations for the leading magazines that must run into the thousands.

What little pleasures and luxuries he allowed himself were confined to his favorite outdoor pastimes—gunning with his friends in the marshes and uplands, rowing in the regattas with the National Association of Amateur Oarsmen on the Schuylkill River, or workouts at the Philadelphia Fencing and Sparring Club, of which he was a member.

After the initial success of *Out of the Hurly Burly* and before he was age 30, he had already illustrated the following additional volumes:

1876—*One Hundred Years a Republic* by Daisy Shortcut and Arry O'Pagus
1876—*Elbow Room* by Max Adeler (Charles Heber Clarke)
1877—*Almost a Man* by S. Annie Frost (his sister)
1877—*American Notes and Pictures from Italy* by Charles Dickens
1879—*Random Shots* by Max Adeler

In 1875 Frost was working on the *New York Graphic* and the following year entered the studio of Harper & Brothers under the tutelage of Charles Parsons who had early gained lasting fame as the delineator of so many of the Currier & Ives clipper ships. Interrupted briefly by a year studying and working in London in 1877–78 and by his studies at the Pennsylvania Academy of Fine Arts, his tour of duty in the Harper's art department spanned more than a decade during which time he worked side by side with E. A. Abbey, C. S. Reinhardt, John Alexander, Thure De Thulstrup, Granville Perkins, Howard Pyle (at whose wedding Frost was best man), E. W. Kemble, Frederic Remington, and numerous other well-known artists.

Frost made lasting friendships in London where he came under the wing of George H. Boughton who had acquired a reputation as a fine painter following an early career as an illustrator. The two subsequently corresponded for many years during which time Boughton alternately offered him severe criticism as well as sincere encouragement. Another great friendship was made with the illustrator Fred Barnard who was himself at the time acquiring the reputation as the logical successor to famed British illustrators Cruikshank and Leech. Barnard's letters to Frost, most of which are illustrated with brilliant sketches, are priceless gems of wit displaying an unforgettable warmth of character.

While in England Frost put forth a few efforts of his own that are worthy of mention, most notably the set of illustrations for Charles Dickens' *American Notes and Pictures from Italy,* of which he was co-illustrator with Gordon Thompson for one edition, and with Thomas Nast for a second edition.

The most significant part of Frost's trip to London came, however, one cold foggy morning when the postman left the following letter in his mailbox:

THE CHESTNUTS, GUILDFORD, Jan. 7/78

DEAR SIR,

Excuse the liberty I am taking in addressing you, though a stranger. My motive for doing so is that I saw a page of pictures, drawn by you in "July" last month, on "the Eastern Question" as discussed by 2 bankers, which seemed to me to have more comic power in them than anything I have met with for a long time, as well as an amount of good drawing in them that made me feel tolerably confident that you could draw on wood for book illustrations with almost any required amount of finish.

Let me introduce myself as the writer of a little book (*Alice's Adventures in Wonderland*) which was illustrated by Tenniel, who (I am sorry to say) will not now undertake wood-cuts, in order to explain my inquiry whether you would be willing to draw me a few pictures for one or two short poems (comic) and on what sort of terms, supposing the pictures to range from $5 \times 3\frac{1}{2}$ downwards to about half that size, and to have about the same amount of finish as Tenniel's drawings usually have.

Believe me
faithfully yours,
C. L. DODGSON
[Lewis Carroll]

It had already been 13 years since the appearance of Carroll's immortal *Alice's Adventures in Wonderland* and six years since publication of *Through the Looking Glass,* both volumes brilliantly illustrated by Tenniel. Were not Lewis Carroll and John Tenniel as inseparable as tea and crumpets?

If, after reading the famous author's letter, Frost had not already seen examples of Tenniel's illustration we can be sure he soon took steps to familiarize himself with the British illustrator's technique. Many years later Frost's library was found to contain a rather worn copy of *Aesop's Fables,* published in London in 1868 and illustrated by John Tenniel with the bookplate sticker of Arthur B. Frost pasted inside on the flyleaf. Whether Mr. Frost or Father Time was responsible for the worn binding, it appears obvious that A. B. Frost was paying careful attention to Mr. Tenniel's methods of illustration. And so was Mr. Tenniel watching his new rival, A. B. Frost!

In a letter to Frost dated February 7, 1878, Carroll mentions that he had shown Tenniel a copy of Frost's first book illustrations in *Out of the Hurly Burly.* He writes:

. . . But I sent the book, at the time, to my friend Mr. Tenniel for an opinion: and I think I may, without breach of confidence, copy what he said. I would not do it if it had been written in a harsh tone, but I think it will not wound your feelings, and possibly, now that you have reached a higher level, you will agree with some of his criticism. He says: ". . . The designs of Mr. A. B. Frost appear to me to possess a certain amount of quaint and grotesque humour, together with an *uncertain* amount of dexterous drawing, which might no doubt be developed into something very much better, but which is at present—as it seems to me, judging by the book—somewhat crude and commonplace in execution; but the pictures are obviously very slight, and perhaps it is hardly fair to give an opinion—"

Tenniel's severe criticism left Frost undaunted and Carroll and Frost, together, in voluminous correspondence of which much spanned the ocean after Frost's trip home, planned the illustrations for the first Lewis Carroll book illustrated by A. B. Frost— *Rhyme? and Reason?* — which was finally published by Macmillan and Co. in London in 1883.

While alone in London, Frost had had a chance to do some careful thinking about both his career as well as his future, and he had been given the opportunity to compare his own artistic merits with those of his English colleagues. Convinced that he needed further study and instruction, Frost returned home, more dedicated to America than ever, and thoroughly convinced of the part his native land was to play in his future work.

Although few, if any, portraits are known to have been painted by Frost, the influence of his distinguished teacher, the renowned portraitist Thomas Eakins, affected his figure work tremendously. It was around this time at the Pennsylvania Academy of Fine Arts that Eakins' life classes created a storm of controversy over his studies of nude male and female figures with the object of achieving perfection in portraying the muscular development and movement of the body. It was under Eakins that Frost perfected his great draftsmanship in the articulation of the body movements and was able to portray so successfully muscular tension or relaxation in his subjects.

Opening a studio at 1330 Chestnut Street in Philadelphia, Frost plunged immediately into illustrations for his third book for Max Adeler, *Random Shots*, plus the big backlog of work which had accumulated during his trip abroad. Several hunting trips to Swift-water in the Pocono Mountains with his friend Norris De Haven followed, including one major but unsuccessful hunting and sketching trip to Canada which pointed to signs that Arthur B. Frost—whose heart longed for Philadelphia—was not long for this world as a bachelor.

Miss Emily Phillips, a lovely petite lady, just a year younger than Frost and herself an artist, was doing part-time spot assignments for *Harper's* when their paths crossed and romance ensued.

Emily Louise Levis Phillips, who became Mrs. A. B. Frost, was born Jan. 19, 1852, just one year and two days after the birth of her husband. She was the daughter of Moro Phillips, a wealthy Philadelphia industrialist, and she had been named after her mother. Emily Frost's great-grandfather, James Ash, had been a notable Philadelphia gentleman

[29]

in the early 19th century. A portrait of James Ash painted by the distinguished early American portraitist, John Neagle, is a prized family possession today.

Prior to her marriage to A. B. Frost, she had studied art in Germany at Dresden and Pillnitz and her skill advanced to a professional level of excellence.

Social customs in America in the early 1800's were rather stiff and formal as is evidenced by this bit of early correspondence from Frost to his future bride:

DEAR MISS EMILY

I send you herewith the book I promised you. I should have sent it much earlier but I have been out all day and have not had a chance before.

I had a very jolly row this morning. The River was rather rough but the air was bracing and fine and I enjoyed it very much and feel very much better for it.

I hope you are feeling very bright and well today and that you enjoyed your drive this morning. I thought I might perhaps see you on the way down to the river. I left too early this morning (9:00 A.M.) to see you on your way up.

This is certainly a most vividly interesting note; don't preserve it in lavender or have it printed for circulation as a model note.

Very sincerely yours
ARTHUR BURDETT FROST

Biographers of 19th century and earlier subjects have many things to be thankful for. In those days without telephones and modern means of communication, letter writing was profusely practiced. Not only did people write many more letters but they were saved and bundled together and, in the case of artists like A. B. Frost, many were illustrated with priceless little sketches:

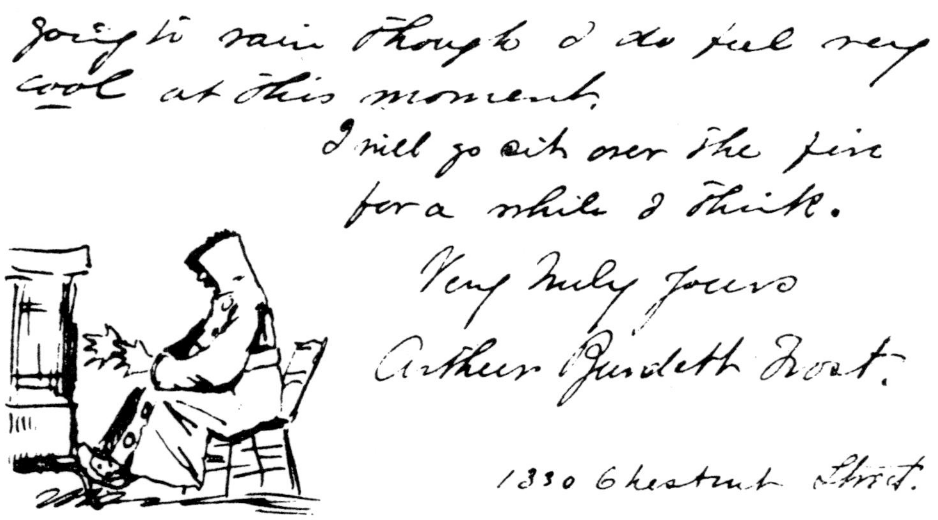

§6. Sketch on a note to Emily Phillips by A. B. Frost.

My dear Miss Emily

I should very much like to walk over to the Depot with you this afternoon and will call for you a little before seven o'clock.

I do not think it is going to rain though I do feel very *cool* at this moment.

I will go sit over the fire for a while I think.

Very truly yours
Arthur Burdett Frost.
1330 Chestnut Street.

In 1883, not long before they were married, Emily Phillips and A. B. Frost were together, among the illustrators of the book *New England Bygones* by Ellen H. Rallings, published by J. B. Lippincot. Miss Phillips' artistic talent, not to be outdone by her now well-known fiancé, was attracting a little attention of its own, though in a slightly different way, as evidenced by this communication from a *Harper's* reader:

Madam;

. . . I have been much interested in studying your picture in the last Harper's Weekly entitled "The Apple Harvest." The general detail and execution of the picture are so pleasing to me that I cannot refrain from calling your attention to one defect, viz.: the impossibility of carrying a basket of apples with so little apparent effort as the girl in the foreground is making. The apples would weigh at least fifty or sixty pounds . . .

They were married on October 19, 1883, and set up housekeeping in Huntington, Long Island, so as to be close to New York. Arthur had now joined ranks with that growing band of commuters on the Long Island Railroad.

✳ CHAPTER THREE ✳

The Golden Age of Illustration

IN THE EARLIEST days of American colonial times the majority of illustrated books were those imported from England. In the latter part of the 18th century a few scattered American publishers had begun printing books with many illustrations. In 1787 an edition of *Little Goody Two-Shoes* was published in Worcester by Isaiah Thomas with a frontispiece credited to John Bewick.

During this period a New York physician, Alexander Anderson, was experimenting with wood engraving and, in 1795, he contributed 37 woodcut engravings for the book, *The Looking-Glass for the Mind; or, Intellectual Mirror*, published by William Durell of New York. Anderson, who became known as the "father of wood engraving in America" remained for nearly 50 years the leading figure in this technique of book illustration.

While Charles Keene, George and Robert Cruikshank, Sir John Gilbert, and two or three others were acquiring reputations as important illustrators in England, practically no illustrator of stature appeared on the American scene until the 1840's when F. O. C. Darley's work first appeared. Darley's work, which shows that he was influenced by Cruikshank, first appeared in 1843 when it was published as a series of scenes of Indian life from studies he had made on a sketching trip to the West in the early 1840's. He had little time, however, to pursue his early interest in the West as his illustrations found their way into volumes by Washington Irving, James Fenimore Cooper, Nathaniel Hawthorne, Henry Wadsworth Longfellow, Lord Tennyson, John Greenleaf Whittier, and many others.

In 1859 another fine illustrator came on the scene—Winslow Homer—who was destined to become one of the greatest American artists. Homer's career as an illustrator was brief, however, and his principal work in illustration was his Civil War scenes of soldiers, infantrymen on the march, and army encampments. Homer went on later with brush, canvas, and water color to the great achievements for which he is remembered.

With the exception of Darley and Homer, American illustration around 1870 was generally erratic and of undistinguished quality, although thoroughly American in flavor in its spirit and subject matter. It had been just a few years since Charles Parsons had left the firm of Currier & Ives, where he had been a lithographer and contributing artist, and had joined the art department of Harper's. Soon Parsons became head of the art department and was responsible for the illustrations in Harper's magazine, *Harper's Weekly*, as well as those in books published by the firm. Parsons assumed the responsibility of hiring and training artists and his technical knowledge and his own talent, particularly as a painter in water colors, soon created a staff of young artists practically all of whom eventually became famous. There was C. S. Reinhardt, senior member of the staff and an extremely capable artist; Edwin A. Abbey, who went on to fame in England as a Royal Academician; J. W. Alexander, who went on to become a distinguished portrait painter; and, of course, A. B. Frost. Not long afterward, the unforgettable Howard Pyle joined the staff at Franklin Square, together with W. A. Rogers, T. De Thulstrup, F. Hopkinson Smith, W. T. Smedley, E. W. Kemble, the great Western artist Frederic Remington, and many more equally important.

Thus began the "Golden Age of American Illustration" which lasted for the remainder of the 19th century and well into the opening years of the present century, roughly corresponding with the career of A. B. Frost, perhaps the outstanding figure of this period. It can be said without conjecture that this era in the history of American art began with Charles Parsons and his young staff in the dingy lofts of the Harper's art department in Franklin Square.

The year 1883 was busy for A. B. Frost! Not only was it the year of his marriage, but house hunting and the thousand and one details attendant thereto, kept him busy enough, without the rapidly growing backlog in his studio. In addition to his staff work on *Harper's* he illustrated, in just this one year, the novel *Hot Plowshares* by Albion W. Tourgee, *Dialect Tales* by Sherwood Bonner, and he finally completed *Rhyme? and Reason?* by Lewis Carroll, which was published in London with 65 illustrations of his own and nine by Henry Holiday. Upon publication, the British author presented Frost a copy of the book with the following handwritten inscription on the half-title page:

ARTHUR B. FROST
from the author
in token of his sincere regard
and grateful remembrance
of the Artist's hand
which had made this book
what it is

Later, while working in his studio to complete five of the illustrations for Theodore Roosevelt's *Hunting Trips of a Ranchman*, Frost received the following letter from the well-known hunter, author, and future president:

422 Madison Ave., New York, Feb. 26th '84

Dear Mr. Frost,

The fifth picture that I want is one I think peculiarly in your vein.

My cousin once wounded a buffalo which climbed up a very steep bluff; my cousin clambered after it, got his hands over the top and raised himself on them only to find the buffalo fronting him with lowered head two yards off. My cousin is a bearded man with spectacles and I have always thought that his face at that moment must have been a study. What do you think of making a picture out of that? It could be called "Tete-a-tete."

The buffalo, with lowered horn advancing, on a flat plateau, with cliff receding at left, and my cousin head and shoulder resting on his elbows and rifle in one hand appearing above edge. I will send you his photograph if you wish it, but it does not seem to me necessary, a bearded man with spectacles, and wild astonishment in his face. Write me what you think of it; before beginning it could I not see you?

Most truly yours,

Theodore Roosevelt

Needless to say the illustrator followed his author's wishes and "Tête-à-Tête" appears just as Roosevelt described it on page 250 of the book which was published by G. P. Putnam's Sons in 1885.

His work for *Harper's* was progressing nicely, too. He writes to his fiancée during their house-hunting days just prior to their marriage:

New York, July 11, 1883

Dear little woman,

Things are just booming; I haven't been in such a good humour for fifteen years. First, Mr. Parsons was *very* much pleased with the drawings. Thinks they are the best things I have done yet. He said a good deal about them and was very complimentary. Says he thinks I am getting the real thing for illustration. Next my comic page was a big success. They laughed over it a great deal and want a lot more as soon as I can do them: next, I got thirty dollars for the two comics, which wasn't so bad as they took me about three hours to do. Next, they want me to draw cartoons for them; offer me a mighty good price and will give me every help they can. We will talk it over and you must think about it; it will certainly pay me over a hundred dollars a week and leave me time for other things, but we will talk about it.

Next, Mr. Parsons likes my idea for Prag very much and urged me strongly to stick out for a copyright, not to let them have anything to do with it without a copyright; he thinks it is a first rate scheme.

Next I saw Mr. Batchelar and he is a very nice fellow I should say, a plain man, printer. Found him setting type in his shirt sleeves. He took a fancy to me from my letter and lamented very much that he had rented his house but he has another and is going to show it to me next Saturday. He will build us a studio, but I find Jamaica is three miles from the water. We might as well live in Montclair, but I will go look at the place anyhow. Next, Mr. Parsons is going to drive me all about next Sunday week and knows of one place that must be lovely, but he thinks the rent is way up and out of our reach.—I have had a most successful day, dear

Love, and feel very jolly. I am more pleased with my work than I can tell you. I think Mr. Parsons was very much pleased and looks for big things from me. He was very kind and nice and wants us to come out his way to live very much. I can see that plainly—

Frost and his bride were very happy and comfortable in their Huntington, Long Island, home. The Sound, with its duck blinds and good snipe shooting, was nearby, and he also had a chance to continue his favorite pastime of rowing. His fellow art student from the Pennsylvania Academy of Fine Arts, Augustus S. Daggy, who was to become one of Frost's closest lifelong friends, lived nearby and the two spent hours together sketching and painting the dunes and shore-bird haunts. It was here that Frost and Daggy, easel to easel, worked happily together. Here Frost painted a charming little sketch inscribed, "Aug. 22nd 1884, First Attempt in Oil," and the Daggy family of Norwalk, Connecticut, have almost the identical scene on canvas painted by their father, also dated 1884.

At about this same time he was working on his second book for Lewis Carroll, *A Tangled Tale*, his first book for Theodore Roosevelt, *Hunting Trips of a Ranchman*, and his own first book, a delightful volume of comic sketches and verses entitled *Stuff & Nonsense*, published in New York in 1884 by Charles Scribner & Sons and in London by John C. Nimmo.

The book was an immediate success, having been published simultaneously on the two continents. Demand for it was so high that it was reprinted again in 1887. The second edition was apparently enormously successful, too, and today, that second edition, with certain revisions, is much more difficult to find than the first.

Fred Barnard, well-known English artist and illustrator, wrote to Frost in December 1884:

. . . We have all enjoyed it immensely—the children were clean doubled up at the first start by the "cat" episode—and I can honestly assert that I have never laughed so much at anything of that same kind—the "qualms" coming on is enough to tick one off, to say nothing of the rollicking yarn to follow—the Kangaroo is Devilish good—In fact the book is a scream from beginning to end . . .

George H. Boughton, National Academician, and close friend of Frost when they were in London together, wrote in January 1885:

. . . your book has been a very great success here— One small shop told me they have sold over 80 copies and that was before the holidays. Abbey told me about it before it was much about and I knocked off and got me a copy at once—he likes it enormously and I think it one of the best of all funny books—You are one of the few who carry *good drawing* all through distorted objects—most misguided folks think any kind of drawing will do for caricature— Mistake!

I like you in this book far better than in your more serious work such as yours in the Xmas *Harper's* where the work looks careworn and "tight," notwithstanding the evident pain you have taken to get it into shape. Excuse my free criticism but I know you *want* to be as perfect as I should like to see you—and as I don't spare myself—why should I you?

§7. "The Fatal Mistake—A Tale of a Cat," pen and ink (1884). This series of hilarious drawings is from Frost's *Stuff & Nonsense*. Those reprinted here are from a revised edition of the original and differ slightly.

So—let yourself *go!* When you draw carefully and don't suffer from artistic constipation. I have said enough—(Pass on!).

So unforgettable were the *Stuff & Nonsense* sketches that 40 years later in 1925, Frost received the following handwritten comment in the lower margin of a formal business letter from a Boston art publisher in response to a routine subscription mail order.

Were you the perpetrator of "Our cat takes rat poison?" If so, I should personally feel guilty in taking any money from you. I laugh now at the memory of that cat's expression as it dawned on her something was not quite right with her "tummy." And calves not flapper's, but onery barn yard ones—I have a farm and no one put more expression in a calf's legs than A. B. Frost. I think you must be the guilty one.

Artists have always been a very fraternalistic group. The idea of jealousy or competition between them has been virtually nonexistent; a spirit of camaraderie and close lasting friendships had developed in New York City around late 1877. Groups met periodically in each other's studios, comparing notes, discussing their techniques and work until someone finally suggested that they formalize their meetings into a club. For a basis of activity each member was to bring a tile to the meeting at which time a design was painted on the tile, which was subsequently oven fired and permanently glazed. "The Tile Club" was thus born.

The club always had something of the air of mystery about it. The meeting place was known only to its members who numbered just 12. The club had no officers, no dues, and no expenses other than rent. Members were to bring their own tiles, cheese, tobacco, and crock of cider. It is assumed that each contributed to furnishing the studio meeting place which was a quaint comfortable "inner sanctum" with a warm fireplace and the atmosphere of the old dark-wood paneled library of a men's club. Each member, upon entering the clubroom, dropped his own name and assumed a different one, probably one chosen as most appropriate by the members.

Frost was known as the "Icicle," E. A. Abbey was "Chestnut," Frederick Dielman, the painter and one time National Academy President, was "Terrapin," William M. Chase was "Briareus," Augustus St. Gaudens, the "Saint," J. Alden Weir was "Cadmium," George Henry Boughton was the "Puritan," F. Hopkinson Smith was the "Owl," C. S. Reinhardt was "Sirius," and so on.

The members met on Wednesday evenings, although not always painting tiles, the time was spent pleasantly in discourse on topics of the day and general relaxation. The club location has always remained a mystery and it is recorded that many who sought to "crash" a Tile Club meeting spent many hours wandering around the dark alleys of the lower west side of New York City. Since telling the "secret" now, almost a century later, will violate no confidences it can be revealed that the club's headquarters were located adjacent to Abbey's studio, somewhere in a cellar alley behind an impressive wrought-iron gate at $58\frac{1}{2}$ West Tenth Street.

As a monument to their existence, or more truthfully probably to raise some money to pay their club rent and other disbursements, the members wrote and illustrated their own work, *A Book of the Tile Club*, published by Houghton, Mifflin & Co. in 1886. The book is an impressively bound de luxe edition with phototype plates by William M. Chase, Elihu Vedder, Frank D. Millet, George W. Maynard, Arthur Quarterly, R. Swain Gifford, C. S. Reinhardt, E. A. Abbey, Napoleon Sarony, J. Alden Weir, F. Hopkinson Smith, Alfred Parsons, Frederick Dielman, and W. G. Bunce.

Frost contributed 12 masterly line-drawing vignettes, and other drawings were contributed by George H. Boughton, Stanford White, and Augustus St. Gaudens.

F. Hopkinson Smith, author as well as artist, who contributed a large part of the text of the book, was probably its instigator. He writes to Frost:

NEW YORK, December 6, 1886

MY DEAR FROSTY:

In cleaning out my pockets (old coat) I find a letter from you dated Nov. 10th.

I don't know whether I ever answered it and I don't know whether you can read this as I now answer it. I had a kind of an idea that you would come tumbling up my ricketies and warm your toes at my hickories, but you didn't.

And I also remember that I left word with my waitress that if a tall fine looking young man with the air of a million (millionaire) rang my tinkler, you were to be shown up into my den, and the fire punched, and a certain glass stopper taken out of an old Venetian Decanter, and a cracker provided, and the New Book laid in your lap and you to be left quietly alone—But you didn't come . . . 'Tis ever thus (Byron).

All Tilers contributing to the Tile Book get the book free—the other cusses pay $12.50 ($\frac{1}{2}$ price). Yours will be sent to "Shocken" [Conshohocken]. But not yet—for the first edition was gotten out under such a pressure that some of the moss types are bad and so the 2nd edition is reserved for the Tilers—It will be ready about Xmas.

Meetings are going on fine,—drop in on us.—

Thine Always
OWL

In 1892 the "Owl" honored the Tile Club again by making it the subject of the entire second chapter of his book *American Illustrators*, published by Charles Scribner's Sons. Chapter 2, "A Night at the Tile Club," reads like the minutes of a Tile Club meeting in which the members are criticizing and discussing each other's techniques. A considerable portion deals with a Tile Club discussion of their colleague, Frost ("Icicle"). It says in part:

The Doctor, who was always a welcome guest, and who always managed somehow to drop in during the evening, was standing with his back to the fire—a favorite attitude—holding in his hand a copy of one of the month's magazines.

"I tell you, gentlemen," he said, "for all the qualities which go to make up a caricaturist in the best sense of the word, we have no man among us who can hold a candle to your own member, A. B. Frost. Now, look at this sketch. Here are a series of drawings descriptive of a cat that has swallowed rat poison by mistake. Watch the expression in its eyes, as shown here in number one, when it discovers the character of the food. Note the wondering look on its face and the slow movement of its paw across the stomach. Only a dot and a line, and yet there is a whole volume of anxiety, alarm, misery, and fright expressed in this same dot and line—one no larger than the head of a pin, and the other no longer than its point. That is what I call genius. Now follow the series through, and note the humor that Frost gets out of the dilated tail and glaring eyeballs in number two, and the final sketch in which the cat, having bounded under the nursery bed at last lies stretched out upon the floor, the two children above backed up against the wall, their toes doubled under them in deadly terror over the unknown cause of the domestic cyclone."

"That is because he is an American," said a Tiler. "When you come to broad humor, neither the Englishman, Frenchman, nor German—I will not even except Busch—understands its intrinsic quality so thoroughly as an American. The merit of Frost's work lies in the fact that he not only appreciates the humorous side of a situation when suggested by somebody else, but, being personally one of the funniest men alive—a perfect mine of spontaneous humor—he adds just enough of his own to make the humor of the other irresistible. You give him the slightest hint of a situation, and before you have elaborated the details he has built the scene all up in his own way into something infinitely more effective. When you add to this gift a pencil which obeys him absolutely and understandingly, it is no wonder that he gets his results."—

"But you would not," said another, "consider Frost only a caricaturist. His illustrations of Ruth McEnery Stuart's 'Golden Wedding,' published in 1889, disproves that. Negro life has never been better expressed on its dramatic side. And do you remember his sketches of camp life and the drawing of the darkeys going to the dance, shuffling along the snow-covered road, half-frozen with the cold, their violins and banjos tucked under their coats? In the delineation of this line of subjects Frost is without a rival."

"I agree with you," said the Doctor. "But you have not exactly hit upon the peculiar quality of the man. What makes Frost so inimitable to me is his genuineness. This is as apparent in his work as it is in the man himself. Everything he conceives, everything he executes is based upon some positive, undeniable fact. . . .

". . . Now run over in your mind every genre painter or caricaturist you ever saw or heard of, and you will admit in five minutes that, even if you are ignorant enough to condemn Frost in his conceptions, treatment and execution, you will be forced to admit that his results are absolutely unique. He is A. B. Frost and nobody else."

With the approach of their first child, the Frosts felt the need of larger quarters. He had always harbored an inner desire for a taste of farming, and since Mrs. Frost preferred to be nearer her family in Philadelphia, the Frosts moved to West Conshohocken, Pennsylvania, and named their new home "Prospect Hill Farm."

On December 11, 1887, their first son was born and, of course, he was named Arthur B. Frost, Jr. Having already contemplated the responsibilities of parenthood, Frost Sr. was up to his neck in the midst of farming his little country estate in the Philadelphia suburbs and producing a massive output of drawings for *Rudder Grange*, his first book for Frank Stockton, *The Story of a New York House*, by H. C. Bunner, and *Ogeechee Cross-Firings*, by R. Malcolm Johnson.

Frost seemed now near the height of his illustrating career. His drawings for Stockton's *Rudder Grange* were acclaimed as his most delightful work to date and marked the beginning of his long-time friendship with the great New Jersey author.

The Frosts spent a good portion of their summers at Beach Haven and the Atlantic

City area of New Jersey. Mrs. Frost particularly liked the shore, while A. B. frequently spent the day sailing, rowing, or in hunting ducks and snipe. He did a large volume of water-color and oil sketches in the surrounding area—beaches, dunes, and the duck marshes which he enjoyed so much. In the fall he hunted woodcock and grouse on his own farm property, with occasional hunting trips with Norris De Haven into the Swiftwater or Bushkill areas of the Poconos.

In 1889, because of another approaching addition to the family, the Frosts decided to move to larger quarters in the vicinity of Morristown, New Jersey. After a thorough search of the Morris County area the Frosts bought a large country estate on Treadwell Avenue in Convent Station and the family moved there in the summer of 1890.

❊ CHAPTER FOUR ❊

"Moneysunk"

THE SIXTEEN years that the Frost family lived in Convent Station, N.J., were the happiest years of their lives. For A. B. Frost, these were the years during which he did his most important work for which he is most remembered.

"Moneysunk" was a very appropriate name for the new Frost homestead. The main house was really a mansion—very large and stately, situated on a little hill overlooking its 120 acres and barn. The mansion had been built late in the 18th century on a campsite of the Continental Army by André Boisaubin, a Frenchman. The house still stands and is a New Jersey historical point of interest. One of the large hollow columns from the porch to the roof of the mansion still contains a stairway used to smuggle slaves from the attic, down the pillar stairway, and into an underground tunnel (now blocked off), which led to a barn some 300 feet away. In Civil War times the house was thus used as a station on the "underground railroad."

The old house and the country surrounding it still looks very much the same today as it did 75 years ago when the Frost family bought it. Old Morristownians will complain that the surrounding country has been built up by developers and garden apartments, but riding through the area you can still see the large estates, horse farms, split rail and stone fences, rolling unspoiled countryside, and iron gateways reminiscent of the noble splendor of the yesteryear that is too rapidly disappearing. Treadwell Avenue, where the Frost homestead was situated in Convent Station, is still an obscure quaint little country road; even the trees seem to be still in place and one cannot help but get a feeling of nostalgia just roaming around the area where the artist worked and lived with his family.

Frost spent most of the summer of 1890 living in "Moneysunk" alone, getting the somewhat rundown mansion ready for his family, which now included their second son, John. Apparently major repairs were needed to get the house habitable, for his letters mention his numerous difficulties with the plumbers, painters, and masons. He writes to his friend Augustus Daggy:

> The studio is going up; the frame is nearly all up and I think I can use it by August first; I am making some changes in it which will improve it, I think. It will be like the last one, the hottest place on the farm, but I can't help that.
>
> How would you like to come rusticate with me and eat chops and raspberries? I can fit you up a room in great shape, and will be delighted to have you.
>
> I am very sorry I could not get Anshutz's book done for him, but I have not touched a pen yet. I am out all day, going from one job to another, and am needed, I tell you; such damnable stupidity as these trained mechanics show is wonderful.
>
> Mrs. Frost and the babies are very well, and very comfortable—Good! Won't I be glad to get them here!!—

After they were finally moved in and organized in their new home, Frost plunged into the midst of a massive output of illustrations for important volumes. That year saw him complete a set of 146 text line drawings for Richard K. Munkittrick's *Farming*. Munkittrick, incidentally, lived in nearby Summit, N.J. Next he tackled the illustrations for his second book by his friend and close farm-neighbor, Frank Stockton, *The Squirrel Inn*.

Frost and Stockton, both of whom were strictly amateurs when it came to farming, had a constant running joke between them regarding their prowess with plow and field. If someone asked Stockton about Frost, he'd reply that Frost was one of the best fellows and best artists in the world—but no farmer. On one occasion Stockton said: "Why, he tried to sell me what he called a first-class horse last summer, and you could hear his joints rattle when he walked. Besides he is no judge of cows."

Frost allowed that Stockton was the best of neighbors and wrote fine stories, "but he's no farmer. He offered to sell me one of his first-class cows, and I had to ask him whether a set of false teeth went with the cow, before he saw that I would not buy her. Besides, Stockton is no judge of horses."

Even at this comparatively early stage in his career Frost had long since acquired the reputation as "a master draughtsman." His earliest drawings for *Out of the Hurly Burly* in 1874 were done in pen and ink on wood which was then cut by the engraver so that the printing could be done right from the original wood block. At this early age this was one of the few methods of reproduction for illustrations available and it was natural that Frost's concentration was in simple line drawings. As a matter of fact his earliest drawings showed the "economy of line" principle which was born, I'm sure, more for the benefit of the poor eye-weary woodcut engraver, than for the quality of the drawing itself. Frost's illustrations in *Almost a Man* (1877) particularly demonstrate this principle, and it is fortunate that the tedious woodcut process was superceded by more scientific methods within the next 10 or 15 years. During this same period the quality of his work seemed to improve in direct proportion to the improvement in the mechanical reproduction process. His line drawings in Munkittrick's *Farming* (1891) or in Joel Chandler Harris' *Uncle Remus and His Friends* (1892) particularly point this out.

Frost first started at about age 25 in working with water colors and wash drawings in gouache, which is an opaque medium with the pigments mixed with water instead of oil. Most illustrators then working in water color or gouache did not use color but worked instead in tones of black, white, and gray or sepia, inasmuch as the reproductions were limited to black and white anyway.

Frost showed great skill in this medium and, aside from thousands of pen-and-ink line drawings, his principal medium for illustration was gouache in black, white, and sepia.

A lot has been said and written about Frost being color-blind. While this is essentially true, Frost had a great feeling for color values. In his black, white, and sepia wash drawings the tones, light and shadows are so delicately and skillfully applied that the viewer many times is almost unaware of the fact that color was not used in the drawing.

In true water colors some particularly fine work was done during the period 1879–84. Perhaps it was "because he was in love" and romantically inclined, at this stage in his life, or perhaps more because these particular water colors were free from illustrative intent, that they are so sensitive and charming. On his trips to Swiftwater and Bushkill, Pennsylvania, around 1880 and to the Canadian wilderness in 1883, his water-color sketches direct from nature are little masterpieces of romantic charm, with colors delicately, almost timidly, applied. He was certainly dreaming of the then Miss Emily Phillips when he painted during this period and it shows in his brush.

Frost would often slip into periods of hard illustration which he later referred to as his "cast iron" period. At these times he would work and rework over a drawing, always a magazine or a storybook illustration, trying to get it "just right," until it tended to lose some of the feeling of spontaneity of his better work. Always, it seemed, he would emerge quite miraculously from this era of hard illustration, usually after a refreshing layoff or relief from a pressing deadline.

His first work in oil—a nice, delicate, but otherwise unimportant little sketch—was done in 1884, yet less than a year later he painted a striking canvas, a magazine illustration, combining many of the attributes of a skillful technician and a romantic impressionist.

In letters to his closest friends, he only rarely showed any satisfaction whatsoever in any phase of his painting; usually he would fret about a "dismal rut" he was in, yet his work was getting better and better. After his initial successes on canvas we find more and more work was done in this medium, including illustration in black, white, and sepia. At this stage, early in his marriage, the young artist was still struggling for financial security, so that the pressure of painting and drawing for money was prevalent.

An amusing incident took place one summer evening in Convent Station while he was sketching a landscape which tickled Frost so much he later protrayed the story in a cartoon. Said Frost: "I was trying to paint a sunset, and, having made a failure of my sketch, I scraped it off the canvas and told a farmer who had been watching me for some time that I had not worked quick enough to get the effect. After some consideration he replied, 'Wal, why don't two or three of yez go at it at onct?' "

By the time the family was settled in Convent, and the financial pressures were at least momentarily somewhere in the background, Frost started thinking about his own true artistic ability. He also wanted his two sons to become fine painters some day and he knew he should start them when they were still young. He felt, too, that he could now take a little time and study again under one of the masters. And what a choice! He became a pupil of William Merritt Chase who was one of the most successful American impressionists and a respected teacher. *Life* magazine, in its issue of July 23, 1965, showed reproductions of two of Chase's paintings and mentioned exhibitions which included his works in New York and the West Coast.

Frost wrote to Daggy, early in 1891:

I have started painting with Chase and I think he will do me a power of good. He will get me to loosen up my blamed tight fist, and get some go into my work. I feel sure he can do me a great deal of good. I like Chase, both personally and artistically, his last summer's landscapes, painted in Central Park, are beautiful. No "purple fad" business, but full of air and out-of-doors.

About a month later, he wrote Daggy again:

I am going to Chase every Tuesday and Chase really seems to like what I do. He told me last Tuesday that I was *painting*. He said "that is painting that is not straining." I have a great respect for his knowledge. He certainly knows a lot that a painter ought to know. He started a picture of Carmencita today, or expected to. It is a commission, and I think he will make a good thing of it. He is right in the humour for it and so is Carmencita. She is to dance at his studio on Monday evening, and I am going in to see her; quite a swell affair, given by some Nabob in New York, Chase asked me. He has a splendid portrait of Whitredge. One of the best heads I ever saw; fine and strong and good color.

I hear the Water Color is very good, and that Smedley is particularly good. I haven't seen it yet. The Academy in Philadelphia is strong, too, has that fine portrait of Sargent's of The Mother and boy.

I am, as usual, driven wild by my work. I am doing Broadway for Scribner's and in a devil of a hurry. I never seem to get time to do decent work, always in a rush. This is the last article on hand, and I mean to make it the last for some time. I have a lot of schemes and mean to try to carry some of them out, painting a little now and then.

Again to Daggy, February 19, 1891, he wrote:

I went to the Water Color Annual Supper on Saturday night and had a very good time, saw all "the boys" and enjoyed it. Bob Ingersol made a bully speech all about Art. He knows less about art than he does about Hell, but he made a mighty good speech all the same; it is a great thing, that gift of "the gab," when a man can talk entertainingly for 20 minutes about something he doesn't know anything about—what must he do when he is on a theme he does know something about. . . .

§8. "A Summer Landscape," oil on canvas (1891). This was painted just a few months after Frost began studying with William M. Chase, renowned American impressionist painter and teacher.

§9. "Daybreak of the Marshes," oil on canvas (*c*. 1900). This was probably intended as a background study for a duck-hunting scene.

§10 "Moneysunk," Convent Station, New Jersey (1890). Frost and his family moved into this handsome old country house where, for 16 years, the artist spent the most productive period of his long career. RIGHT: "Moneysunk" as it stands today. (Courtesy of the New Jersey Historical Society.)

§11. "Bicycling in the Snow," gouache (1898). This painting depicts Frost and his two sons during their happiest years in New Jersey and reflects the then contemporary bicycling craze.

§12. A. B. Frost and his sons in the studio at "Money-sunk" (c. 1903).

§13. "I Reckon I Got to Be Excused," gouache (1896). The illustration, which shows Tom, Huck, and Aunt Polly, is from Mark Twain's *Tom Sawyer Abroad, Tom Sawyer Detective, and Other Stories.*

§14. "I Could Hear Similar Explosions As He Went Down the Road," gouache (1900). This was reproduced originally as the frontispiece for the August 1900 edition of *Scribner's* Magazine for the Sydney Herman Preston story of *The Green Pigs*. The wash drawing was later made into a print for a portfolio, "Pictures from Scribner's."

§15. "A Big Order for the Church," gouache (1906).
Reproduced in *Collier's* Magazine, April 7, 1906.

§16. "Easter Eggs—the Source of Supply," gouache (1905). Reproduced in *Collier's* Magazine, April 8, 1905.

§17. "Where the Ruffed Grouse Lie," water color (*c.* 1890).

§18. "Old Copper," oil on wood panel (*c.* 1900).

§19. "The Copper Jug," oil on wood panel (1902).

Later in the same letter, in an obvious reference to "still life" painting of the usual pots and vases on table tops under instruction from his teacher, William M. Chase, he wrote:

> I am becoming quite the pot painter. I paint pots and pans at Chase's 'til you can't rest.

Under Chase's tutelage Frost improved greatly. His canvases lost the tell-tale minute detail trade-mark of the illustrator and developed a free-flowing style and a keen perception toward tasteful composition. Although Frost would have been the very last artist in the world to consider himself impressionistic in any way, his oil landscapes give one the feeling of exuberant freedom from the hard confines of illustration. He chose surprising numbers of still-life subject matter to paint and his canvases give one of the best impressions that he was enjoying his work tremendously.

Nevertheless Frost still had a tremendous backlog of illustration ahead of him, and his most important work in this field was still yet to come before he could give it up to become a painter.

"Brer Rabbit" and "Uncle Remus"

FROST'S FIRST illustrations for a Joel Chandler Harris story appeared in *Century* magazine in 1884 for the short story "Free Joe and the Rest of the World," an appealing story of a slave in which, to use Harris' words, "I have striven merely to recall to the memory of some of my friends the unhappy environment of one of the Lord's creatures." Frost contributed four line drawings for the story; whether he was illustrator at the author's request or did the assignment at the request of *Century* magazine, for whom he occasionally did free-lance work, is not known. Perhaps Harris had noticed Frost's illustrations a few years earlier in Sherwood Bonner's *Dialect Tales*. However, we know that the two did not meet until 1886, as shown in the following letter from Harris to Frost:

March 19, 1886

MY DEAR MR. FROST:

I really hope I didn't make an unfavorable impression on you by reason of any lack of conversational tact, and my general lack of fluency. I have no social accomplishments whatever, and avoid society in all of its shapes and forms as one would shun the plague. The knowledge of this deficiency—or, rather, of those deficiencies embarasses me to an extent beyond description. But for the fact that my house is disarranged by a lot of paper hangers, I should have offered Mrs. Frost and yourself the hospitalities of my home, such as they are.

I had intended to drive you about over the city yesterday afternoon and still hope to have that pleasure—and the pleasure of your company in various other ways; for I feel sure, after what I have written that you will not misunderstand what may have seemed want of consideration if I may attempt an awkward description of a keen appreciation of my own shortcomings; I write this fairly because I don't want you to misunderstand my awkwardness nor mistake it for coolness or carelessness; and I can write it so much better than I could explain it orally.

I have a hundred things I want to talk to you about—among others the illustration of a little volume of "Plantation Songs and Ballads," which Scribner has been advertising as in press. I want, also, as you know, to make three or four trips with you to the mountains— especially on the Marietta and North Ga. road. I think you would enjoy it and you could make others enjoy it, particularly if you would allow me to write a running account—half humorous and half descriptive—of the trips as a sort of string (poor string!) on which I hang your sketches.

If you will give me a day's notice, I will be ready for the Mountain trips at any time that may suit your convenience. Meanwhile, come down and talk to me. I don't want to miss the opportunity of seeing as much of you as possible.

Faithfully yours
JOEL CHANDLER HARRIS

Whether the two ever did get together for their trips into the north Georgia mountains is not known. However, Frost's sketchbook from this period shows some studies of a cotton gin in Marietta, Georgia, and there is also a charming water-color sketch inscribed, "Warm Springs July 27 '86."

A little later the two collaborated on a short story entitled "Little Compton" which appeared in *Century* magazine, April, 1877. Frost contributed six pen-and-ink line drawing text illustrations to the story which dealt with community life in the middle Georgia town of Hillsborough.

Also in 1887, *Free Joe and Other Georgian Sketches* by Joel Chandler Harris was published by P. F. Collier & Son, with Frost contributing the frontispiece as the book's sole illustration. The first "Uncle Remus" story to be illustrated by Frost, however, was still five years away.

The correspondence between the two, published here by courtesy of Emory University Library and the Joel Chandler Harris Estate, becomes more voluminous in 1892 and seems to portend something important in the offing between the two:

May 30, 1892

MY DEAR FROST:

Instead of answering your letters as I ought to have done I have been hurrying up with the Remus stuff, and I will send it to you as soon as I can have a copy made. You are placing me under great obligations, Dear Mr. Man, and I thoroughly appreciate it. I enjoy your work whether it is humorous or serious, and the Cow and the painter in Scribners came near putting me to bed. I laughed till I was as sore as an amateur baseball club in the suburbs. I want you to illustrate the matter *in your own way*, which is preeminently the American way. We shall then have real American stuff illustrated in real American style. Be as comic as you choose, or as commonplace as you choose—you can't possibly fail to please me. There's this consolation; if you can't find fun in my stuff, you've got it in your bones, and fun is what we're after. Thank heaven! We're both red-headed.

I've been trying to find out whether I can accept your kind invitation but I can't tell yet. Some of our people will have to go to the big conventions. After that hullaballoo settles down I'll let you know. I'd like to see those boys! Of course they take after their mother; and equally of course she says they take after their Pa; but they don't, do they? Think of having Jack Frost all summer, and only two pairs of slippers in the house to warm things up! My

§20. "Free Joe," pen and ink (1884). This drawing illustrated
Joel Chandler Harris' "Free Joe and the Rest of the World"
(*Century* Magazine, November, 1884).

§21. "Brer Rabbit," pencil sketches (1892). From these early beginnings evolved the unforgettable image of Brer Rabbit for Harris' *Uncle Remus and His Friends.*

§22. Adventures with Brer Rabbit, gouache (1895).
These two illustrations from an early edition of the
Harris book on Uncle Remus show the mischievous Brer
Rabbit in a couple of comical situations, most notably
his encounter with Tar-Baby.

oldest will be 18 in June, consequently I'm beginning to feel gray in the mind. He's reporting on an afternoon paper falling into the business in spite of all I could say.

My regards to Mrs. F. I know she must be happy with those boys—not counting her old man (which is Georgia for husband).

Faithfully & gratefully yours,
JOEL CHANDLER HARRIS

The principal subject of their correspondence was, of course, the book which became the immortal American literary classic, *Uncle Remus and His Friends*, published by Houghton Mifflin in December, 1892.

Publishers must have been fast workers in those times, for as late as October 1st, 1892, Frost wrote the following in a letter to his close friend, Daggy:

DEAR OLD MAN:

I have been trying to get over to see you, but I am so blamed busy I haven't had an afternoon to spare lately. I am doing a book for Uncle Remus, and am not getting ahead very fast with it, but I *am* making good drawings, which is better. I wish you could see them before they go in. I think they are about the right thing for the subject. I enjoy making them very much.

Later in the same letter, he closes:

. . . Do come over, old man. I can't leave till I get these drawings done and that will be ten days from now at least; I would like to show them to you.

It is obvious Frost was enjoying his assignment of illustrating the book of "critters" for the great Southern author. Harris' charge that "I want you to illustrate the matter *in your own way*" must have been refreshing enough, but his suggestion to "Be as comic as you choose, or as commonplace as you choose" were probably just the words Frost needed to inspire him to his best effort.

Rarely, do any of Frost's letters to family and friends show any satisfaction whatever with his work. Usually he was so rigidly self-critical that he would consider himself in an interminable rut; however, in this letter to Daggy he displays unusual enthusiasm.

His sketchbooks for the period, most of which are now contained in one of the distinguished libraries in the state of Georgia, where they rightfully belong, are replete with studies of rabbits, their heads, ears, noses, some dressed in human clothing and in various poses—sitting, standing cross-legged, smoking a pipe, and various other poses which were to become familiar to millions of Americans.

Harris, at the time editor of the *Atlanta Constitution*, was understandably delighted with the red-bearded Northerner's illustrations, and he makes no effort to hide his pleasure in the following animated letter:

December 15, 1892

MY DEAR FROST:

I am almost as bad as you are about writing letters. The fact is, I have been waiting with impatience that package of sketches which, a month ago you were to send *to-morrow*. My dear Mr. Man, your head is red and so is mine, and, on this account there is much to be forgiven. Need I tell you that I am delighted with the illustrations? The only fault I find with them—and it is an irremediable—(is that a sure enough word? it looks might funny)—one, is that they are too few by a couple of dozen. They are simply perfect. The humor of the lion looking in the spring and showing his tushes stays with me, and de big black gal is a gem. Bless God! She's de gal her own se'f, done come out'n de cotton-patch an got dar on de paper right fo' yo' eyes.—I send with this a picture of my own, which I have named "Rough on Rats."—In my Editorial about you I made one curious omission—I said nothing about your Western characters in Miss French's stories. A mighty slick gal, that Miss French.—Of course I should like to spend a week or two with you, and see the wife and those notorious boys, and Frank Stockton. But how can I? I'm the slave of the Editorial grind. I like Frank Stockton. There's no nonsense about his writings—that is to say, there *is* nonsense about and in his writing, but no nonsense about his style, which reads like the talk of a clever, friendly man talking before a cosy fire, while waiting for the taters to be pulled out of the ashes and the simmern beer to be brought in. Now then, *when* are you going to send those preliminary sketches? Or did you change your mind? My regards to Mrs. Frost, and the boys, and a Merry Christmas and a happy New Year to you all!

Faithfully yours

JOEL CHANDLER HARRIS

The book contained three full-page wash drawings and nine pen-and-ink line drawings. If Harris felt the illustrations were "too few by a couple of dozen" he certainly saw to it that this situation was soon corrected. Shortly after this first Frost-illustrated "Uncle Remus" appeared, the decision was made to publish a new and revised edition of the original *Uncle Remus, His Songs and His Sayings* which had first appeared in 1880. This time it was illustrated by 112 A. B. Frost drawings and it was this issue that contained the open letter by the author to Frost in the preface and dedication which says, in part:

. . . it would be no mystery at all if this edition were to be more popular than the old one. Because, by a stroke here and a touch there, you have conveyed into their quaint antics the illumination of your own inimitable humor. . . .

The book was mine, but now you have made it yours, both sap and pith.

Said the *New York Tribune*, November 17, 1895:

. . . Mr. Frost's sketches for the new edition of "Uncle Remus." They are delicious. No other word will do. Technically they exhibit the fine maturity of Mr. Frost's art, his tact in the handling of line, his fineness in matters of color, his skill in making his pen as eloquent as a brush and in giving to black and white designs the solidity and the variety of paintings in oil . . . But technique is soon forgotten in the contemplation of these drawings. They are fun incarnate . . . Their costumes are irresistible. Their attitudes are indescribable—But the only thing to be said of the work as a whole is that it is screamingly funny, the most brilliant piece of humorous characterization which has been done in the history of American art.

From the *Evening Post*:

. . . One goes about the gallery smiling, or talking to total strangers about the drawings and the tales they illustrate. Certainly a kinship exists between Mr. Harris and Mr. Frost to a delightfully sympathetic degree. . . . One departs from the exhibition inwardly wondering who is the more fortunate, Mr. Harris in having his inimitable work so perfectly interpreted, or Mr. Frost in having so joyous a theme to celebrate.

Several more books followed—all important—but to consider them here with the indelible classic image of the immortal Brer Rabbit stuck fast to the Tar-Baby in our minds is anticlimactic. The editors of the *Tribune* and the *Evening Post* have said it all. Harris and Frost had written together one of the greatest, most unforgettable classics of American literature.

The final exchange of correspondence between Harris and Frost deals with *A Book of Drawings by A. B. Frost* published by Colliers in 1904, consisting of 40 full-page drawings of genre subjects, rural characters, barnyard and hunting scenes. The book became one of the best loved, most typical works of A. B. Frost. Joel Chandler Harris contributed a warm and eloquent introduction to the book. Verses to accompany each drawing were written by Wallace Irwin, decorated with pen-and-ink vignettes by the artist. The following two letters were the last written to Frost from Harris and deal with the introduction to the book:

September 20, 1904

DEAR FROST:

You will have to excuse the typewriter—it is such a little one—and it is much closer to me than a pen. It spells comfort for me since my illness, and it is the only kind of writing that affords me any pleasure.

I received a letter from Mr. Clinton a few days before yours came, and shortly afterwards a dummy of the book they propose to get out. Honestly, now, do you suppose that I, who know nothing of the technicalities of art, can do justice to the extraordinary way in which you reproduce character in your drawings? It is a great gift, and only one man out of ten thousand has it. If you really think I can do justice to that gift, I shall be glad to undertake the preface for Collier's. You will have to aid me a little with a few points about your personality —though I had rather have Mrs. Frost's views on that matter than yours. If you can imagine eyes sharp enough to see the red meat in an uncut watermelon you will know how a woman— especially a man's wife—can see and get at the real essence of individuality. Therefore, if you can get Mrs. F. to give an extemporaneous pronouncement on the man Frost, I shall be obliged to you.

I am sorry to hear that the little lady is not feeling spry enough to travel; and I can sympathize with her thoroughly. I have a constant home-feeling that I can't get over. I have an uneasy feeling even when I get away to some little Georgia town. I know just how a setting hen feels when she is driven away from her nest.

Otherwise it would be the greatest pleasure in the world to accept your kind invitation.

Down here everything is pretty much as you left it, with the exception of some material improvement that doesn't count. Business is knocking all the romance out of the young men; they cut their hair short, and no longer go about with dreamy eyes. You'll see in the newspapers a good deal about Georgia and the negro—the poor darky never does get a fair deal when politics are hot. But politics never bothers me except in the way of vain regrets that people old enough to know better should make fools of themselves over nothing in particular.

Faithfully yours,

JOEL CHANDLER HARRIS

Kindest regards to Mrs. Frost and the boys.

October 1, 1904

MY DEAR FROST:

I wrote you a letter some time ago, in response to one from you. A day or two afterwards Mr. Clinton sent me a telegram stating that whatever I proposed to write should be sent on so as to be in the office of Collier's Weekly one week from the day the telegram was sent. So I went out and found a pick-axe, a spade and a derrick and proceeded to build in a hurry what is probably one of the most inane introductions that was ever put on paper. I cannot write in a hurry; when I try the journalistic side of my mind comes to the front and takes charge. On the other hand, when I have ample time, the literary side of my mind will slowly turn over, bur its eye, cuss because it has been waked up, and then proceed to do what I want it to do.

I am writing to beg you not to allow the introduction to appear unless it is perfectly agreeable to you; and if you desire to suppress any part of it, seize it by the ears, and run your blue pencil through it.

Faithfully yours,
JOEL CHANDLER HARRIS

§23. "Upland Bird Hunting," gouache (*Scribner's*
Magazine, November, 1916).

§24. "Grouse Hunting," gouache (*Scribner's* Magazine, November, 1916).

§25. "Woodcock Shooting," gouache (*Scribner's* Magazine, November, 1916).

§26. "Fly Fishing," gouache (*c.* 1903). Much rarer than his shooting scenes, this painting shows another sporting activity in which the artist found much enjoyment.

§27. "Golf—Dormy Two," gouache (*c.* 1898). Depicting a "new"
sport taken up by Frost, this painting which first appeared in
Scribner's Magazine was later reproduced in the portfolio, "Pictures
from Scribner's."

The Sporting Pictures

OVERSHADOWING almost all of his other works, collectively—including even the Uncle Remus illustrations—A. B. Frost is most well remembered today for his hunting and shooting scenes, particularly those of men with gun and dogs. Collectors of sporting art are increasing rapidly in numbers today. Galleries handling sporting art exclusively have sprung up in many of the principal cities. From the slow beginnings of the 19th century, hundreds of sporting books have been published in the last half-century and they are being eagerly collected by bibliophiles of sport. Rare sporting books are fetching high prices at auctions, and important sporting libraries have come into existence at leading universities, most notably at Yale and Princeton.

Leading galleries are conducting exhibitions of sporting art exclusively, and of great importance is the fact that many of our present fine artists in all fields have made important contributions to this field. Great masters such as Winslow Homer, George Inness, Albert Bierstadt, and even our greatest portraitist, Thomas Eakins, have all created important examples of sporting art. Arthur F. Tait, the great Adirondack and Western painter of the latter part of the last century, was one of our earliest notable sporting artists.

Fanny Palmer, who shared Currier & Ives fame along with A. F. Tait a century ago, is our most famous woman artist in sport and her quaint colorful woodland scenes of well-dressed gentlemen with six-foot-long shotguns and ill-proportioned dogs fill hundreds of curly maple frames in the old print shops and homes of antique collectors in this country and abroad.

Outstanding sporting artists of the last few decades include Frank W. Benson, N. A.

(National Academician), Roy M. Mason, A. Lassell Ripley, Roland Clark, Ralph Boyer, Edwin Megargee, Marguerite Kirmse (the fine woman artist who drew dogs so well), Lynn Bogue Hunt, Eric Sloane, and dozens more. Perhaps the greatest living sporting artist is Ogden M. Pleissner, N.A., whose pictures, sporting and otherwise, are found in the finest collections and museums. Pleissner is regarded as one of our greatest living water colorists. His fishing and hunting scene prints made for the Anglers' Club of New York are classics and are among the rare and unobtainables today.

We submit just a smattering of names in this field—dozens more should be mentioned and the subject of sporting art in America is a worthy topic for a book. Regardless of who or how many should attempt it, there is one name that will always be at or near the head of the list of the great sporting artists America has produced. It is, of course, A. B. Frost.

Dozens of artists have surpassed Frost in technique, in handling of color, and in true artistic merit; yet why is Frost regarded as the finest of them all? The answer lies in the fact that Frost, himself a sportsman, is able to translate to the eye of his viewer the exact feeling which is taking place within his subjects in the pictures themselves. He captures the instant of suspense and excitement as the bird is about to flush, or the ducks are about to "stool in" over the decoys. Frost was a stickler for correctness in detail. The hunter's clothing is perfect, right down to the corduroy collar on the canvas jacket and the buckle on the boot. Perhaps even more remarkable are his dogs. There are two scenes in particular: one showing a hunter and his dog starting out on their day's shooting, and a second scene shows the same pair at the end of the day. In the first, the hunter and dog are full of pep and anticipation and seem to walk with a spring in their step. In the second scene they are tired but contented after the long day in the woods and fields. Just by the way the hunter's foot touches the ground or the way his hat is on his head tells the story. With the dog it is the entire body, head, his tongue and even the droop in the dog's tail.

The autumn hunting scenes are classics of correctness. In spite of his color blindness, his autumn colors are particularly pleasing to the eye.

Much has been said and written about this phase of Frost's work. Sporting galleries throughout the land always seem "sold out" of the Frost pictures and prints. In the past few years costs of the shooting pictures have increased dramatically and their availability has all but disappeared.

In 1890, interest in the game of golf, which historically had its origin in Scotland in the late 15th century, was spreading rapidly and within just a few years golf courses with large impressive clubhouses were springing up in the wealthier suburban areas.

Around 1895 the Morris County Golf Club came into existence. The club was scarcely more than an easy 15-minute walk from "Moneysunk" and A. B. Frost took up the new game of golf with vigor. Some amusing stories are told of the redheaded artist's bursts of temper and antics on the golf course with partners Robert Foote and W. G. Van Tassel

Sutphen who was later to become Rector of St. Peter's Church in Morristown. One event in particular recalled with amusement by an older club member is an outburst by Frost, angered at himself over a poor shot, who exclaimed, "You redheaded s—o—b—." Soon afterward, he discovered his caddy, whose red hair he had not noticed earlier, had dropped his bag and stalked off the course.

Beginning in 1895 he started doing series of golf drawings for *Harper's*. There is a set of six large wash drawings depicting scenes of members at play on the Morris County Golf Course, and the originals of those drawings are now proudly displayed in the main reception room of the clubhouse; in the trophy case can be found a trophy won by A. B. Frost himself in one of the club's local tournaments in 1896.

In 1898 Frost and golf partner Sutphen collaborated in writing a marvelously funny book of golf sketches entitled *The Golfer's Alphabet*, published by Harper and Brothers in both New York and London. Sutphen wrote a jingle for each letter of the alphabet, which Frost illustrated. The two collaborated again from time to time in short stories and sketches for the leading magazines.

It would be wrong to assume that the emphasis in Frost's sporting art was shifting to the new fad of golf away from his now familiar hunting scenes. His sketchbooks of later years show evidence that he was continually experimenting with new ideas and studies for shooting pictures. His golf drawings from this period, practically all of which were assignments for *Harper's* magazine, do constitute an important contribution to the pictorial history of this sport in the country. Many of the better ones appeared again as full-page plates in the portfolio "Sports and Games in the Open"; however, those presently hung at the Morris County (New Jersey) Golf Club are the most important from this period.

There were three main groups of Frost's sporting prints published. The first was the series of 12 colored lithographs published by Charles Scribner's Sons in 1895–96 known as the "Shooting Pictures" portfolio. The next important group of prints was the set of six lithographs in color published by Scribner's in 1903 and known as "A Day's Shooting." Finally, there was the set of four hand-colored copper plates published posthumously in 1933–34 by the Derrydale Press and limited to 200 copies. At various times there were several other printings in black and white of sporting as well as genre subjects but the three aforementioned groups of sporting prints in color were the most important. Another publication of importance was "Sports and Games in the Open" published by Harper & Brothers in 1899. This portfolio, which is extremely hard to find today, consists of 60 plates in black and white of various sporting subjects, including hunting, fishing, golfing, and bicycling. Frank Stockton contributed an eloquent introduction to the publication.

The "Shooting Pictures" portfolio of 1895–96, about which so much has been said and written, is easily the most popular and hence the most widely collected item. Certainly the 12 lithographs in color immediately gave Frost his position as our premier sporting artist. Yet Frost himself, in typical fashion, could not be pleased. He writes to Daggy December 2, 1895:

> I have not got these damned shooting things done yet. They drag, and are a mill stone "round my neck," and the reproductions are enough to make a dog sick. . . .

Frost is being ridiculously critical here. In my research on this phase of the story I was lucky to find a 94-year-old man with an amazing memory who worked for Scribner's around the turn of the century. He recalls Frost's visits to the office, usually to pick up his royalty checks. He told me that Scribner's had the complete set of originals for the shooting pictures framed and displayed along with a set of the prints similarly framed and displayed and if one backed away six or eight feet, you couldn't tell which were the originals and which the prints!

He writes to Daggy again in February, 1896:

> We have had a tough time since Christmas. The Boys were taken sick the same day soon after Christmas, influenza. Then Mrs. Frost got it. About the time the boys got well I went down and was sick just a month, in bed over a week, and am only now feeling like myself again. We were pretty blue too, for I worked on those shooting pictures all the Fall, and got no money and we got behind hand; and it wasn't pleasant. We are better off now for I am at work again and there is "mon" coming in.

The "Shooting Pictures" consisted of 12 color plates depicting the most popular forms of upland game and shore-bird hunting of the times. Contained in a large board portfolio, decorated with red imitation leather and red-ribbon tie strings, and with a Frost-drawn English setter's head on the cover, the lithographs were divided into six parts of two plates each, contained in a heavy gray-paper wrapper. A large text sheet came with each color plate, carrying text written by Charles D. Lanier describing each kind of shooting. Frost decorated each text sheet with three pen-and-ink line-drawing vignettes.

Over the years the favorite prints were removed from the portfolios and framed, and the remainder of the clumsy wrappers and tissue sheets discarded. Today it is difficult enough for collectors to accumulate the 12 color plates, but nearly impossible to find the original board portfolio and assemble the fragile wrappers and text sheets.

In 1903 Scribner's again published a portfolio of A. B. Frost's sporting prints, this time entitled, "A Day's Shooting." It consisted of six color plates, comparable in quality but slightly smaller than the 1895 set of 12. There are two duck-hunting scenes, "Good Luck" and "Bad Luck," two upland-game scenes, "Ordered Off" and "Gun Shy," and two charming pot-hunter Gran'pa and Gran'son pictures, "Smoking Him Out" and "We've Got Him." Actually a set of three pairs of prints, it is estimated that no more copies were printed than in the case of the original portfolio some years before which numbered about 2,500. For collectors this is a most difficult set to put together. "Ordered Off" and "Gun Shy," though scarce enough, can be found through diligent searching since they were the most popular and consequently not discarded. "Good Luck" and

§28. "Shooting Pictures," lithographs (1895). These are the famous series of twelve American sporting pictures (pp. 79–89) issued by Scribner's. ABOVE: "Autumn Grouse."

"Autumn Woodcock."

"Quail—a Dead Stand."

"Quail—a Covey Rise."

"Rabbit Shooting."

"Summer Woodcock."

"Duck Shooting from a Blind."

"Duck Shooting from a Battery."

"Rail Shooting."

"Prairie Chickens."

"Bay Snipe."

§29. "A Day's Shooting," lithographs (1903). These six works by Frost (pp. 90–94) were originally published by Scribner's.
ABOVE: "Ordered Off."

"Gun Shy."

"Good Luck."

"Bad Luck."

"Smoking Him Out."

"We've Got Him."

§30. Hunting scenes, copper plate prints, hand colored (1933). This
set of four (pp. 95–98) was printed by the Derrydale Press in a limited
edition of two hundred. ABOVE: "October Woodcock Shooting."

"Grouse Shooting in the Rhododendrons."

"A Chance Shot While Setting Out Decoys."

"Coming Ashore."

"Bad Luck" have long been gobbled up by the duck hunters and are the most popular pair of the set. The last pair, "Smoking Him Out" and "We've Got Him," were apparently the least popular of the set and were probably the first to become lost or discarded, making these prints the hardest of all to find today. When first issued, the set came handsomely packed in a colorful cardboard box with a fine picture of the hunter and his setter on the cover.

Although for a long time overlooked and considered unimportant because they were published after the artist's death, the Derrydale Press set of four A. B. Frost prints published in 1933–34 are easily the most desirable of all the sporting prints to own. Made under the supervision of John Frost, the artist's second son, who himself hand-colored the first impressions from the plates for the other colorists to use as a guide, these were done on the finest imported rag paper and the plates were destroyed after 200 copies were made. Although the original "October Woodcock Shooting" was done by Frost in tones of black, white, and sepia, he had left behind two water-color studies of the subject so that his color impressions are definitely and faithfully translated to the Derrydale print. In the duck-hunting scene, "A Chance Shot While Setting Out Decoys," in the treatment of the reflection of the sunrise on the water and that of the hunter, bundled as warmly as possible and crouching low in his punt, Frost captures not only an exciting instant of the sport but the raw frigid atmosphere of dawn on the marshes. A grouse-hunting scene with an excellent study of an English setter pointing a bird, entitled "Grouse Shooting in the Rhododendrons," plus another duck-hunting picture showing two contented hunters returning with full bags of game, entitled "Coming Ashore," completes the set.

The Frosts Move to Europe

DURING THE last five years he lived in New Jersey, A. B. Frost was at the very zenith of his career. The Uncle Remus illustrations had gained him worldwide fame and the "Shooting Pictures" established him as the nation's finest sporting artist. As an American book illustrator he had already more than 70 volumes to his credit, no less than eight for Joel Chandler Harris alone, with one more yet to come from the great editor from the South. He had just finished his Tom Sawyer and Huck Finn illustrations for Mark Twain at the turn of the century. Practically every issue of *Harper's* and *Scribner's* had his illustrations, either for stories or for color plates.

Certainly at this stage of his career, A. B. Frost had more than fulfilled even the most ambitious goals of any American illustrator. He had reached the loftiest pinnacles of success in his field. Inwardly, however, Frost realized that it was becoming progressively more difficult for him to satisfy his own extremely self-critical eyes which were just now beginning to give him the danger signals of approaching failing eyesight. "Moneysunk," their large stately old homestead with its nearly 130 acres, was becoming more difficult to care for. His two boys, Arthur, Jr., and Jack, were now teenagers and had already shown talent and interest in becoming artists. Frost had their futures to look forward to and, in addition, the desire within him to succeed as a painter was growing strong. He writes Daggy in December, 1903:

> I quite agree with you as to the simple side of life, I wish to Heaven I could get nearer to it. We live very simply, it seems to me, in some ways, but we have too big a place and it costs too much to run it. I have it for sale and I mean to push it for all I am worth. I am sick of it and I want to get away from this lot of money worshippers that surrounds us. We

see almost no society, for we can't keep up the pace set here and don't want to. I am going to get out as soon as I can. I am laying track already and next summer may see us in New Hampshire and next winter in New York. Whether we sell the place or not, I can shut it up and save a lot of money.

Frost, it seems, was being typically self-critical in his letter to Daggy. Although Mr. and Mrs. Frost were not socially big entertainers in the Morristown area, they had a host of close friends among the prominent people in the vicinity and the appearance of the successful and distinguished red-bearded artist caused a stir wherever he appeared. The Frosts were particularly friendly with the Frank Stocktons, Robert Footes, Louis Thebauds, W. Alston Flagg—who advised Frost on financial matters—and the Charles Scribners. Also his pictures had already made their way into the collections of such prominent New Jersey families as the Twombleys and the Frelinghuysens and it is certain that his letter to Daggy did not refer to these people. It is felt that Frost, in his letters to Daggy, would purposely withhold any evidence of his own good fortune from his very best friend who was still struggling to gain his foothold in art. He writes again to Daggy in December, 1905:

This Christmas time is hard on a man whose eyes are not good. I am having more trouble with my eyes, head-ache and nervousness and I can write but little at a time.

Mentioning his boys' futures he tells Daggy that his son Arthur was entered in William M. Chase's art school in New York and that he was also studying with Robert Henri:

I hate to have him spend 3 hours a day on the train but it can't be helped. He likes it very much and likes the school. I am not sure about the teaching there yet, but it will do for a while. I wish I could talk to some of the men who have been through it.

Jack is at school yet and we hope to make about another 18 months do for him. I want to sell or lease this place and go to Paris to live, indefinitely, no plans, stay if we like it, come home if we don't.

I am working hard for Colliers and saving money to live on when we go abroad. I am going to say goodbye to illustration when we go. There will be no brass bands and fuss when we go, but when I go I go out of illustration for good, *I think!* You can't tell, I may be teaching a young ladies school next.

In the summer of 1906 the Frosts finally sold the magnificent old homestead at Convent Station, and, after attending to the thousand and one details necessary to settle their affairs, the family sailed in July for Europe, stopping first in London. In a letter to Daggy, dated August 17, 1906, he writes:

We saw a good deal of London in our week and went to the National Gallery a good deal. It is a magnificent collection in a wonderful gallery. There are some wonderful old Masters, and a great many of them, too... We saw the New Velasquez, the nude "Venus" and a grand piece of flesh painting it is, we just happened on the very last day of the Royal Academy Exhibition and we saw it pretty thoroughly. It was very bad. There were not six good pic-

§31. "A Summer Landscape," oil on canvas (*c*. 1891). This is a good example of Frost's sensitive feeling for nature, as the morning sun penetrates the mist on the meadows.

§32. French landscapes, water color (*c.* 1910). These three studies were done by Frost in France during the period the family lived in Europe.

by my grandfather
AB FROST
John Frost

§33. "A Paris Street in the Snow," oil on canvas (1910).

tures in the 1400 oils, but some very good little water colors. I don't like Abbey's picture and I don't like Sargent's. The English paint just as they did 25 years ago, hard, finished tight stuff, with the same mawkish sentiment, and they all paint alike. Their best men did not have anything good in the exhibition. We went to the Tate Gallery where the contemporary painters are represented by one or two examples of their best work, and there are some very good pictures among them.

Frost fell in love with the English countryside, the "long streets with the finest old cottages and houses on either side and set in beautiful country. We are enjoying it very much. We walk and paint when we can but the weather is so beastly it is very hard to do anything. . . . I wish we could settle in England. It is a mighty fine place to live in, but English Art is too much for me, I couldn't contemplate the prospect of my boys absorbing any English Art with anything but dismay."

Following their original plan, the Frosts stayed only briefly in England, then moved on to Paris in September, 1906. Frost established his studio in Paris, which he shared with his younger son, John. Arthur, Jr. set up a smaller studio in the same vicinity of the city. Frost enrolled both his sons in the Académie Julian for the serious study of art. Frost himself found it rather difficult to get into full swing with his own work. He found the Paris climate with its erratic mixtures of snow, rain, and intermittent patches of sunshine too difficult for him to attempt an important canvas so he confined himself to studies and sketches. He found it was also very difficult to break away completely from illustration. The American publishers and magazines continued to send him manuscripts and assignments, and considering the high cost of the trip abroad with its hotel living and other heavy expenses, Frost was rather grateful for the opportunity to replenish his slightly diminishing coffers. He consoled himself in the fact that he could commence his serious painting in the spring, after the weather settled down in a more consistent pattern.

While in Paris, Frost renewed his friendship with Charles Dana Gibson, the well-known illustrator and perpetrator of the famed "Gibson Girl" whose classic beauty was always portrayed surrounded by hordes of properly attired, handsome young men. Like Frost, Gibson was establishing a studio in Paris for the purpose of concentrating on painting so the two "ex-illustrators" had a real common denominator at this stage in their friendship which was to continue for more than 20 years. Through Gibson, Frost became acquainted with another American artist in Paris, Frederick MacMonnies, noted sculptor and painter. MacMonnies' letters to Frost, which have been carefully preserved, show that the two visited each other often in their respective studios, sharing advice and encouragement.

In the late spring of 1907 the Frosts moved to a country home at Giverny par Vernon, Eure. It was a quaint picturesque little French town, a favorite for artists, just a few hours from Paris by train. They rented a suitable cottage, just a block away from the great French master, Claude Monet, whom Frost greatly admired.

[107]

A. B. Frost was highly pleased with the work of his son, Jack, who had worked hard while studying at the Académie Julian in Paris, but he was becoming increasingly concerned about a trend in the work of his son, Arthur. While in Paris Arthur quickly fell under the influence of the Modernists whose painting abandoned realism almost completely in favor of forms created by the emphasis of color and light removed from description of nature. He quickly rejected the principles of painting so long and traditionally cherished by his father.

The elder Frost had long anticipated his first summer in France as the opportunity to concentrate on his own painting; however, he became deluged with difficulties and Mrs. Frost became quite ill and was bedridden for several weeks. Early in 1908 he writes to Daggy:

> I have absolutely nothing to show for my time, nearly two years. I paint all the time but it is poor stuff and I destroy it all. Last summer was a complete disappointment, but it couldn't be helped. We had to go where it would do Emily the most good. I am counting on this summer to work. I hope nothing will prevent it, with a house in the country I ought to be able to paint something worth while . . .

Frost's inability to concentrate undoubtedly resulted from concern over Mrs. Frost's health, his son Arthur's infatuation with the Modernists, and further difficulties of his own, which by now included a hernia. He writes again to Daggy, in September, 1908; however, his difficulties seem not to be truly serious, and in his letter the typical old-time Frost humor begins to sift through:

> I had planned a lot of work and here I am knocked out of a month, for I won't be able to work for another week and the shooting season has been open ever since I went to bed. I had been looking forward to the shooting all summer as my one chance to get any fun. I haven't had any pleasure since I came to this country, no golf, no anything, and this was to be my chance, it is rotten hard luck. Jack goes out quite often and has killed quite a number of partridges and rabbits. He is not shooting as well as he used to and I think he needs someone to steady him and tell him what he is doing, but he makes some good shots. He got a double on partridges the other day. There is a good deal of game. Jack has seen pheasants and hare and two deer, but did not get shots at them. Deer and boar come quite close in the houses here after the shooting on the preserves opens. We have had pretty good fun, fishing all summer.

Although far from pleased with his work, Frost at this time produced some exquisite water-color studies of the French town, the old stone barns, stone walls, quaint churches, and flower-lined roads and paths. His French landscape studies were done with a sensitivity that captures the feeling and atmosphere of the country. Perhaps one of his very best canvases from this period is a lovely Paris street scene in the winter. The treatment of the slushy snow on the sidewalk along a masonry wall, the impressionistic blending of the leafless trees into the foggy background creates a fine composition of Paris in the winter.

After a few years in France, however, he felt that his painting had not progressed to the point where he could become recognized as much more than an ordinary painter. In June, 1909, he wrote:

I paint, but not with the idea of ever making a painter, I simply get some fun out of it. I find my colorblindness too great a handicap to overcome, even putting aside the other difficulties. I am going to make a book and it will fill my time for all next winter and maybe more. I think I can get some fun out of it, and possibly some money, too. It will be a collection of everything I can do, caricatures, serious figure drawing, bits of old French towns and farm houses, and American country bits, a little of everything. It will be fun to do it.

In the spring of 1911, A. B. Frost's streak of hard luck hit its climax when he discovered that both his sons had tuberculosis. This was a sad and bitter blow to Frost, as the health of his sons was to plague him for the rest of his life. He writes to Daggy:

The main thing at present is that Jack is sick. Too much work in unaired studios and growing fast have used up his strength and he is in bed for a time. I feel anxious about him, he is not strong constitutionally. I am afraid Jack will be on the sick list for some time and his Mother and I are worried. We have had a hard winter in the matter of health. We all have had very bad colds and Arthur still has his, I am just about over mine. I lost three weeks' work, didn't go to the studio in that time and as I have all the illustrating I care to do it was rather a loss . . .

Six weeks later he writes again from the Hotel National in Davos-Platz, Switzerland:

When I wrote you last month about Jack being ill I knew he had tuberculosis, but I did not know the extent of the disease. Soon after I wrote you our physician in Paris consulted the Paris specialist and they decided the best thing to do was to take Jack to Doctor Turban's Sanatorium here in Davos-Platz. We came here with him five weeks ago and he was put to bed at once, and yesterday was the first time he has been up . . .

Arthur looked wretchedly and has had a succession of colds all winter. Dr. Turban examined him and found his lungs were in an inflamed condition and advised him to take a preventive cure. They have taken an X'ray of Arthur's lungs and it confirms their diagnosis exactly. (later)—I am doing absolutely nothing. I will try to get some painting going soon. I was so knocked out and upset by this terrible thing that I felt fit for nothing for a while. I had made arrangements to work for Colliers and Scribners and would have been making a fair income and have a good time, but I have to give it all up for I can't work here. I will have a big studio when we get settled and get to work again.

With both his boys in the sanatorium, A. B. Frost soon got over his bitterness and his morale improved considerably as he watched their progress. He and Mrs. Frost were comfortable in the Swiss hotel and seemed almost to enjoy their stay in Davos-Platz. Although Frost's eyes were now troubling him considerably, he resumed illustrating with redoubled effort since hospitalization expense for the two boys was substantial.

He writes to Daggy, April 19, 1912:

[109]

I haven't been doing much writing lately. I've been trying to save my eyes, or eye, for work. I'm making a book, in caricature. I sent about 20 drawings to Doubleday Page and Co. and they are very much pleased with the thing. I'm taking my time over it and hope to produce something worthwhile. We are getting along very well. Arthur is going back to Paris to live soon. He has an apartment joining his best friends, the Bruces, and will take his meals with them. So we feel that he will be watched and if he should not be well we will know of it.

Jack is doing well. He has not had a set back since he came here, which will be a year day after tomorrow.

The book referred to in the letter to his old friend was *Carlo*, published in 1913 by Doubleday, Page & Co. *Carlo* is the story of a dog, a lovable gangling awkward pet who comes to live with a family and Frost portrays pictorially the hilarious antics which take place as the dog romps merrily through the book from kitchen to chicken coop.

Although Frost had continued his magazine and book illustration while the family had been in Europe it had been 20 years since his previous volume of comic sketches, *The Bull Calf and Other Tales*, had first appeared and the public received *Carlo* like a long lost friend.

Said the *New York Sun*:

Ever since A. B. Frost made his bow as a drawer of pictures, which is as far back as most of us can recollect, he has managed to give his animals all the requisite expression without changing their natural characteristics. His beasts may be comical, but they are never caricatures. In an album entitled "Carlo" (Doubleday, Page & Co.) he traces some exciting passages in the life of a plain dog with no pride of ancestry. The pictures tell their own story, with no need of enlightenment from the sparing text; they are as natural, as absurd and firmly drawn as any that Mr. Frost has ever turned out and will be a joy to those that see them.

The *Knickerbocker Press* (N.Y.) wrote:

"Carlo" has to be seen to be appreciated and this is the first appearance, for none of the material in "Carlo" has ever appeared in any form. Those who love children and whose love for dogs and those who love a good joke will find much merriment in this pleasant book of drawings by A. B. Frost just published by Doubleday, Page & Co. Mr. Frost is well known as one of the few artists who can improve on animals and jokes by putting them on paper. Every one remembers his "Brer Rabbit," the "Tar Baby" and all the quaint world of "Uncle Remus." The whimsical drawings of "Carlo" are in the same vein.

Carlo was so popular that a second edition was published in 1924.

With the recovery of his sons from their bouts with tuberculosis, Frost decided to bring to an end the family's hapless journey to Europe. He longed to return to his former simple American country life; he had now abandoned any serious ambition of doing anything but occasional painting. His success with *Carlo* had convinced him that he should stick principally to illustrating. One more disappointment, however, was in store for Frost before he could sail for home. That was the decision of his son, Arthur, to remain in Paris to continue his painting with the French Modernists. Frost took the bad news with typical philosophical acquiesence, nevertheless he was bitterly disappointed about the career of his older son. Finally, in May, 1914, the Frosts ended their eight-year absence from America and sailed for home.

A Family of Artists

BACK AROUND the turn of the century, it was not at all uncommon for one or more members of a family to undertake seriously the study of art or music. Radio, television, and motion pictures had not yet invaded the culture of American family life so it might be expected that parents would attempt to develop the natural artistic tendencies in their children.

It was particularly appropriate and natural that the Frost children should follow their father's footsteps and study art. Their mother, too, remember, was an artist with noteworthy accomplishments.

It is unfortunate that so few examples of Mrs. Frost's work remain, for she, too, began a career of her own as an illustrator for *Harper's* and developed a fine artistic talent. Outside of her oil portrait of her husband which appears in Mr. Lanier's biography, *A. B. Frost, The American Sportsman's Artist*, plus a small, but delightful, unfinished water color and a fine pencil portrait of her husband, no other works by Emily Phillips Frost are known to exist. According to family correspondence she threatened to destroy completely all of her work, however this seems to have been more in jest than a serious threat. Nevertheless, the entire Frost family were artists of the highest caliber and the story of the Frosts as a family of artists now becomes a sequence of brilliant, shocking, tragic, sad, and again brilliant events.

In 1905, about a year before the family sailed for Europe, A. B. Frost enrolled his son, Arthur, in William M. Chase's art school in New York. Arthur, Jr., who had already mastered the basic skills of drawing under his father's tutelage, worked hard and progressed rapidly. So rapidly and brilliantly, in fact, that he was encouraged to study further with Robert Henri, an outstanding artist of the "Ashcan" school and destined to become famous as one of the "Eight" (Arthur B. Davies, William J. Glackens, Robert Henri, Ernest Lawson, George Luks, Maurice Prendergast, Everett Shinn, and John Sloan). The "Eight," also known as the "revolutionary black gang" and the "Ashcan" school, were so called because, unlike their predecessors, they portrayed the unglamorous New York sidewalk scenes—the slums, theaters, prizefighters. They were one part of two distinct movements in American art around 1913, the other being the Modernists.

During this period of the 18-year-old youth's life, he painted a remarkable portrait of his father which is now in the collection of the Philadelphia Free Public Library. Young Arthur's brother, John, had already begun his career, too, under his father's supervision.

A. B. Frost was full of high hope for his artistically talented sons when the family sailed for Europe in the summer of 1906. They were to be enrolled in the Académie Julian in Paris and become fine painters. His plan was simple—with his sons thus busily engaged, he would concentrate on his own painting and abandon illustration completely. He had it all figured out, but he had not figured on the French "Modernists" and the "Salon d'Automne." He writes to Daggy, November 1, 1906:

> . . . Jack is fine; he is very anxious to go to work in the Julian School and I am going to let him—he draws well and is full of imagination, and he is happy in his work. Arthur is causing us great anxiety—listens only to the damned fools who have had something to do with the Chase school. I have seen this contempt for drawing and painting and all technique and it had ended in "impressionism" which was then the refuge of the incompetent.—Paris appears to be full of fools to judge from this Autumn Salon. I can't understand it at all. I laughed the first time I saw it, but not for long, it grew serious enough before I got through the rooms. You can't believe till you see it; as Dana Gibson said yesterday to me "If that is painting, your cook can paint."

A month later he writes again:

> You don't understand about Arthur, evidently, he is making a bad mess of it. He might as well be in Morristown for all he is getting out of Paris, painting impressions of nude models is not the way to learn to draw and paint. He is old enough to go on his own way and I will not be responsible for such foolishness. Jack is going into the Julian School on January first. He is doing very well with me and has advanced quickly with his charcoal drawings. He couldn't work a large drawing when we came here. We are all very well and getting along comfortable. We take French lessons but Mrs. Frost and I are pretty slow, the boys do well. I am making illustrations because I can't paint out of doors. As soon as I can paint I will drop it pretty nearly altogether, only doing what I can do from nature. We will probably be in the country all summer and I will find plenty of stuff to do.

Although A. B. Frost did not realize it at the time, or at any subsequent time in his life, his son, Arthur, was soon to join into the midst of a group of young artists who would play a significant role in the history of modern American art.

[114]

When Frost enrolled his two sons in the Académie Julian in Paris, early 1907, his older son, Arthur, had already been well grounded in the rudiments of art. Arthur had previously studied briefly at the Pennsylvania Academy of Fine Arts (where he had exhibited with recognition) and more intensively under Robert Henri at the William M. Chase School in New York. Although he applied himself diligently to the basic work of the Julian school, the new color movement of the young impressionists had already caught his eye and had captured his imagination.

By mid-1907 Arthur Frost, Jr., had met another young American painter, Patrick Henry Bruce (1881–1936), who, like Frost, had studied under Henri at the Chase school in New York. Bruce had come to Paris in 1904 after a promising beginning when he had exhibited at the National Academy of Design. In Paris, Bruce had continued his early impressionistic flowing style which revealed his Henri training; but by the time the Frosts were arriving in France, Bruce had become infatuated by elements in the new movement in painting and had been admitted to the frequent Saturday-evening salon meetings at the home of Leo and Gertrude Stein who entertained the celebrities in French art. Through Bruce, Arthur Frost met the Steins and gained admittance to the charmed circle where he came under the influence of Henri Matisse and Picasso.

Much to the consternation of his parents, Arthur soon dropped out of the Académie Julian and enrolled in Matisse's school which was just being organized. The elder Frost displays his bitterness in a letter to Daggy in March, 1908:

> Arthur is now working in a school just started by Henri Matisse. He had reached the bottom, he can't degrade his talent any further. His studies are silly and affected and utterly worthless. He will come to his senses too late, I'm afraid.

Three months later Frost again wrote Daggy:

> I am sorry to say Arthur is just the same. I can see nothing in his work but affectation. No one can see nature as he paints it. He can explain that it is a color scheme or some such thing, but he brings home a canvas with a smudge of rank green for a tree with pure black for the stem and some blue for a sky and harsh yellow for buildings. He pretends to say that he sees nature in that way, but as it is the way the whole damned crew of Matisse followers paint landscape, I simply doubt it. Why do they *all* see nature as Matisse sees it? People who follow their own bent in art don't all see alike. It is a dreadful thing to see a boy of his talent wasting his time as he does.

In a letter a month later Frost's contempt for Matisse reaches a near comical level:

> He is a charlatan and a fake and a pretty dirty one, too. He sold Arthur a little panel about 10 inches long that he painted in an hour for $80.00. I think a man who would sell one of his pupils, and a boy at that, such a thing for such a price, is a dirty mean cuss.

It is not difficult to understand the elder Frost's concern regarding the growing tendencies in his son's art. The young Frost was entering a period of transition, by stages, into movements which ultimately became known as Cubism, Orphism, and Synchromism. The young circle of artists who were excitedly experimenting with these principles in art around 1906–16 were creating storms of critical protest. It was yet to be half a century before a sound, sane critical assessment of their work could be evaluated. At the present time the doors of recognition are just beginning to swing wide open for this little band of American artists who, with their now well-known French colleagues of Cubists and Orphists, were laying the very foundations of modern art as we know it today.

So quickly did young Arthur Frost, Jr., grasp these concepts that he exhibited his first painting in the Salon d'Automne in 1907, less than one year after the Frosts had arrived in France!

Young Arthur tried in vain to explain his feelings to his parents; however, so deep-rooted were his father's academic principles that he stubbornly refused to attempt to understand his son. Although the elder Frost, himself an admirer of Renoir and Monet, had felt the liberating effects of Chase and Henri in his own studies with them and had later translated their teachings into his own impressionistic canvases, he still could not accept Matisse as anything but affectation.

At length, young Arthur, unable to embrace completely the rudimentary principles of the Académie Julian and equally unwilling to reject the teachings of Matisse, gave up painting altogether. He began to study in earnest at the Sorbonne. First it was literature, then music—so intensely in fact, that he bought a piano and actually attempted to compose music. Finally, after a long agonizing self-evaluation he returned to painting. Taking an apartment of his own in the same building with his close friends, the Bruces, he resumed his painting in earnest. He writes to Daggy:

DEAR UNCLE GUS:

I can write to you now as I have no more theories and one can write about realities.

I have been through hell's fire and damnation and have come out of it all with an unshakable conviction of myself as a *painter*, a first class painter.

I was in a rotten state and thought I had no gifts just because my gifts weren't somebody else's gifts. Everybody jumped on me. Everything I did the invariable answer was *"dead."* Hearing myself called dead so damned often I began to think and believe I *was* dead and bought pictures of a friend of mine instead of painting them myself, admired those pictures, scorned my own (although I hung some of them on the wall nevertheless). I looked more at my own pictures than at my friend's, but I thought that was just curiosity, to see their faults, such was my confidence in my friend's reasoning. But I never really learned any of this modern academy stuff. I thought that was lack of sensibility in the direction of painting and that not feeling the things I couldn't grasp them intellectually! etc. etc. etc. !!

Well it all blew over through a new friend, a real live inspired man, who brought me an audience by admiring my stuff! He saw its qualities, rough rude strength, straightforward frank painting, admired them, and I saw them! Then all my life of painting was lit up to me and I see now exactly the same quality in a drawing by me in September 1896 as in the stuff I am at work on now. And you bet I am happy! I get up at 6 every morning and go to bed at 9, and I paint. I stick to my paintings like a burr and will continue sticking the rest of my life. I have no theories. I make photographs. I copy nature. Now I see the painters thus

COROT
RENOIR
COURBET
DELACROIX
CEZANNE
SEURAT
    Picasso   Matisse
              Delaunay
              Bruce
(FROST)—the filling out of this name is my job.

I have 4 pictures started and I work on them all the time. Sunlight, morning, white houses and others against key and sea—10 m. afternoon—house with orange roof and vermillion shutters against sky—12F.

Gray morning—Houses against key and sea—15F. afternoon—black pony against grass. (The pony is in colors ranging from ultramarine to alizarme, crimson. He contains also red, greys, and a little black.)

I wish I could see you for you are a painter who paints nature and we are therefore brothers. My love to you and good luck with the motif. Stick to it.

                                Yours ever,
                                ARTHUR FROST

On July 28, 1913, Arthur writes to his mother, from Pouldu in Finistére, France:

DEAR MOTHER:

Pouldu is wonderful and I am perfectly content, well and hard at work. I have started 3 pictures, one early morning gray, one morning sunlight and one afternoon sunlight. All 3 landscapes of modern houses. The sea is in two of them. I intend to work long on all of them. I get up at 6 and go to bed at nine.

There has been one colossal painter in our epoch, Cezanne. Renoir is also all right. I will do like Cezanne the rest of my life, study nature long and intently and see more and more clearly. The weather is warm and perfectly clear.

Interrupted only during the period of Arthur's recuperation from tuberculosis in 1912–13, Frost and Bruce lived, worked, and studied together in close association for nearly four years. Their work advanced in stages beginning earlier with Renoir-inspired impressionism, then transcended through the Matisse influence to Cézanne-Cubist patterns, then to the color principles of Delaunay, and finally to individual expressions of all they had absorbed.

There is an interesting letter from Arthur to his mother, undated but probably written during the period of transition, in which he mentions Cubism:

Last night I went to Mr. & Mrs. Steins. Talked some time with Leo Stein and Pat, about cubisme.

Today I take Bruce to the Colonne concert, at 2:30 P.M.

You wanted to know if the cubists intend that the subject be obscure in their pictures, I tell you frankly *I do not know!* The cubists are called so in bulk, but they all don't paint in cubes, nor is there any one thing by which one can class them as a crowd unless it be the obscurity of the subject. However, one can paint a collection of lines without suggesting some

[117]

object or objects to the mind of the person who sees the picture. Picasso painted a thing which I called, as soon as I saw it, the machine-shop picture. It does look like a machine-shop though it was not meant to look like anything at all.

The term "Synchromism" as a movement in art was actually founded by two young Americans, Morgan Russell and Stanton Macdonald-Wright, who in 1913 exhibited 29 of their paintings at the Galerie Bernheim-Jeune in Paris. This new principle involved a great deal more than the traditional uses of color and light in painting and their exhibit in one of the most prominent French galleries caused quite a stir of criticism and misunderstanding, much of which still continues today.

Although Arthur Frost and Patrick Bruce, as well as Robert Delaunay, who had already begun to have tremendous influence on both of them, never allied themselves with the Synchromists, they, nevertheless, had themselves been experimenting with principles of color and light to the extent that their work was similar to the movement in many ways.

The underlying theory in the work of Frost and Bruce had to do with color application and the principles of contrast and the fusion of colors which produced form rather than the use of lines to produce form. Form was also created by harmonizing together small patches of color gradation. The whole theme seemed allied to the idea that the creation of form would be more forcefully created by intense color blending.

Frost and Bruce, initially tremendously influenced by Matisse, soon abandoned their allegiance to his school and became deeply affected by the great French artist, Cézanne.

It is tragically unfortunate that only one or two examples of Arthur Frost's paintings from this period are extant. His major remaining work, shown at Knoedler Galleries in New York in the fall of 1965 in an exhibition entitled "Synchromism and Color Principles in American Painting 1910–1930" is a very remarkable canvas called "Harlequin." Arthur describes the painting in a letter to his father dated October 22, 1914:

> I liked the horse I did which I wrote you about very much. I have since done a Harlequin (a no. 5) in oil. A figure with his back turned, in tights made like a patch work quilt of all colors. I enclose drawing I made it from, but the drawing is not standing on its feet, the painting is. It is very pretty. I have now 17 things which *go*, ranging from 3 to 25.

Late in 1914, several months after the rest of the family had sailed home for America, Arthur Frost, who at the time was living and painting with the Bruces, managed to get into considerable trouble with the French authorities over a rather trivial incident. He explains it in a letter to his parents, dated December 13, 1914:

> I don't believe I have told you the real story of the arrest and it isn't in the report I made for Conner which I sent to Jack. It was like this. Pat and I went down to the quay on Friday morning to see a batch of German prisoners which had just arrived. We went up a street. We had permission from a sentry armed with a gun and bayonet to follow the line of the curved arrow instead of going all around the block of houses, so as to get on the sidewalk behind the line of sentries. While we were on the guarded ground the military commander came rushing

up and grabbed Pat by the shoulders and shook him hard 3 times. Pat protested and said the sentry let us pass. The Colonel didn't answer and he rushed up to me and said "Allez-vous en d'ici" exactly as one talks to a dog. I stood still, whereupon he said "Voulez vous que je vous fasse en aller de force" I answered "Allez y." He then arrested me.

That is all there was to it.

I am sorry that you saw all those rotten newspapers as I don't pretend always to do dignified and right things and I would not blame anybody seeing those articles for thinking that this time I had acted like a scrub, it was the Colonel who made an ass of himself and acted like a jumping jack.

I never gave any cigarettes to prisoners, except one that an English speaking prisoner asked me for in the boat coming from Nantes. One time in the woods back of our house I gave them some tobacco but in the sight and under the nose even of a French soldier. We never had any prisoners in our house and never talked to any anywhere near the house.

Only during his trial did Arthur realize the extent of his troubles! He and Bruce had apparently been under surveillance by the French on suspicion of espionage and his arrest had simply been a fabricated incident so they could arrest him and put him in jail. His youthful inquisitiveness regarding the German prisoners of war caused him trouble on more than one occasion. In another letter he wrote to his brother, Jack:

It was rather a spooky feeling when that old s.o.b. at Quiberon said he was going to shoot me. I tell you frankly at the time I didn't know but that he might be ass enough to do it and drunk enough. He was drunk. I determined to die game. It was a rotten feeling but gave me an insight into this war business. I just thought "Well, if its all up, its all up, I can't do anything about it. I'll just go out well so that none of my family or friends will be ashamed of me." I didn't sleep a wink that night in the hotel however, altho' by that time I knew I wouldn't be shot. I only thought I would be shot for a few minutes. That was enough, when he told me he would shoot me I was sitting at a cafe table far from the fire. It was cold and I began to shiver. I thought "this old s.o.b. if he sees me shiver will think I'm scared" so I went and stood with my back to the fire right next to the old goat.

Finally on December 14, 1914, Arthur was able to send his parents, who by this time must have been near the end of their ropes, the following cable:

ACQUITTED NEWSPAPERS DISGUSTING ALL DIGNITY ON MY SIDE FROST

Two weeks later, Arthur, greatly sobered by his harrowing experience, and by now more than a little homesick cabled his parents the best Christmas present he could have given them:

SAIL JANUARY FIVE ROCHAMBEAU HAVRE ARRIVE NEW YORK FROST

Soon after returning to America, Arthur Frost set up his studio on East 14th Street in New York City, and applied himself more diligently than ever to painting. He was anxious to produce a truly important painting, embodying all the color principles he had learned in Paris and he was soon hard at work on a very large canvas. He spent several months on the painting, often rejecting and repainting several areas in order to make it achieve exactly the desired result. When the work was nearly complete, he received a shipment of several paintings from Bruce which were to be sold in New York. Seeing Bruce's recent work for the first time in several months, Arthur perceived a new dimension in his best friend's art which harmonized elements of black and white into the color spectrum. This new dimension affected Arthur so strongly that he repainted his canvas entirely, incorporating Bruce's newly discovered innovation. Arthur's painting was put on exhibit by the Society of Independent Artists in 1917, of which he had been made a director.

While in Paris Arthur's life was solely dedicated to advancing his art. While his recreational pursuits had been principally confined to the type of activities conducive to the recovery of the tubercular patient, his activities in America gradually and progressively became just the opposite. Late in 1917 his Bohemian dissipation climaxed itself and he became violently ill. Scorning medical assistance, he died very suddenly on December 7, 1917, four days before his 30th birthday.

Writing in *Scribner's* magazine in May, 1918, Walter Pach said in his article "Arthur B. Frost, Jr.":

> The passing of a young artist, full of life and rich in promise as he was, might not seem an event capable of arresting attention for long, in times like these when great numbers of young men are being swept to a death whose reason we cannot comprehend,—at a time also when one of the greatest sculptors of the modern world and one of its finest painters have gone from among us. But it was precisely because his career was unfinished, because he had gone far along a course that might have yielded results defining the thought of our day and of its immediate morrow, that the death of Arthur Burdett Frost, Jr., came as a grievous shock to all who knew him or his work.
>
> . . . The results were evident by 1913 when we find young Frost as one of a group of painters—Delaunay was probably the most prominent of them—who had their own word to say. They were all men who had the scientific-aesthetic research of recent years well in hand, they had passed the groping state in getting a balance between realistic and abstract form, and their pictures of aeroplanes, clouds, the sun and other heavenly bodies were part of the movement of creative art for which our time will be remembered.

A. B. Frost never completely recovered from the shock and grief of his son's death. His sadness remained with him for the rest of his days. There is no record of family correspondence for almost one year following Arthur's death, no letters to Daggy, just a blackout. The mystery of the whereabouts of Arthur's painting is unsolved. The "Harlequin" is the only finished canvas from Arthur's peak period extant. Two examples of Arthur's earlier French painting are in a private collection; the Philadelphia Free Public Library owns the remarkable portrait the 18-year-old boy did of his father, and a few minor examples of Arthur's work as an early teenager remain with the family. At the time of Arthur's death a young painter, James Daugherty, now of Weston, Connecticut, maintained a studio near young Frost. Daugherty had felt the impact of the new treatment of color principles in art and he subsequently made significant contributions of his own to the new movement. Daugherty owns a large unfinished canvas by Arthur Frost, but it is so incomplete it is important only because it demonstrates the methods used by the artist during the earlier stages of the work.

Outside of these examples mentioned nothing else has turned up. The whereabouts of the large canvas exhibited in 1917 at the Society of Independent Artists is a mystery although a suspicion remains that his father, shocked and grief stricken, went to his son's studio to clean up his personal effects and destroyed everything.

§34. "Harlequin," oil on canvas (1915). This is a painting by Frost's older son, Arthur—one of the few surviving works from the peak period of the young artist.

§35. "The Blue Bowl," oil on canvas (*c.* 1891). This was probably painted during the period Frost was studying with William M. Chase.

§36. "The Shepherd and His Flock," gouache on paper (c. 1895).
Because this is a radical departure—in a free expressionist manner—from
the usual style of Frost, it always arouses unusual interest from art
students and critics whenever it is exhibited. It displays Frost's great
versatility and expressiveness when freed from the confines of illustration.

§37. Portrait of A. B. Frost, oil on canvas (1906). This portrait of the artist is by A. B. Frost, Jr. (From the original in the Rare Book Department of the Free Library of Philadelphia.)

§38. Portrait of A. B. Frost, oil on canvas (c. 1920). This portrait of the artist is by John Frost, the younger of his two sons. (From the original in the Rare Book Department of the Free Library of Philadelphia.)

※ CHAPTER NINE ※

Back Home in America

ARTHUR'S BROTHER John, younger by three years, had had a much more severe case of tuberculosis and he spent close to three years in Dr. Turban's sanatorium in Davos-Platz until his release in the spring of 1914. Prior to his sickness Jack had worked hard at the Académie Julian and had also studied with National Academician Richard Miller who was in Paris in 1908–9, and who had painted a fine large portrait of A. B. Frost which now hangs in the Pennsylvania Academy of Fine Arts in Philadelphia.

Frost wrote the following to Daggy in June, 1909:

> The man Jack worked with last winter, Richard Miller is here and I want Jack to work with him down here. Jack is doing excellent work, he has a fine color sense and paints very well. He is really serious about it, too, works hard and shows steady improvement. His strongest bent is for landscape, but I think the figure will come later on. His figure work last winter was very good and he was very much interested in it. I want him to work on the figure out of doors with Miller and he will later. The men here take Jack's landscape work very seriously and treat him as if he were an arrived artist instead of a boy. He does mighty good work.

Although Jack's work showed steady improvement, his health began to deteriorate and finally resulted in a diagnosis of tuberculosis. Only during the latter part of the three years spent in the Swiss sanatorium did he resume any semblance of serious art study.

As soon as Jack was released from the sanatorium in April 1914, the Frosts, except for Arthur who had elected to remain in Paris with the Bruces, sailed for home.

After the inevitable and joyful reunions with the Daggys, Harpers, Scribners, Doubledays, Dana Gibsons, and the other artists, as well as the hosts of friends around Morristown, the Frosts made a motor tour of New England, principally western Massachusetts as well as the shore areas of Connecticut and Rhode Island, looking for a country home. They finally settled in Wayne, Pennsylvania, a suburb of Philadelphia in a "large airy house with high ceilings on a hill surrounded by trees."

In October 1914, the Society of Illustrators gave a homecoming, testimonial dinner in honor of A. B. Frost. Here is a report of the affair as it appeared in the *New York Morning Telegraph*, October 17, 1914:

> Three hundred members of the Society of Illustrators from all parts of the United States, attended a dinner given to A. B. Frost, dean of American Artists, at the Hotel Brevoort last night. Charles Dana Gibson, president of the society, was toastmaster, and in the only address of the evening referred to Frost as the most venerable artist in America and said that he well deserved the distinction of being known as dean among them.
>
> Moving pictures, illustrating many of the older cartoons and sketches of Frost were shown. "Dizzy Joe," a comic sketch which was first published in Scribner's Magazine several years ago and resulted in a series of tramp sketches by Frost, was enacted before a moving picture camera and reproduced last night. Winsor McCay made several sketches of "Gertie," showing the antics of a dinosaurus, and also of "Little Nemo."
>
> James Montgomery Flagg was shown in the character of Si Stebbins, Will Foster and David Robinson made up the Bull Cow, Charles Voight and Louisa, a mule, George Kerr, a cat and Willard Fairchild, a dog.
>
> Among those present were Frank Doubleday, Alexander Harrison, Dan Beard, J. W. Alexander, Peter Dunn, Arthur Scribner, Rose O'Neill, originator of the Kupie dolls; Lady Duff Gordon, Mary Wilson Preston, Walter Trumbull, Djuna Chappel Barnes, Grantland Rice, C. Allen Gibson, Thomas E. Hardenbergh, C. D. Williams, Montague Glass, Harry Dart, Arthur William Brown, George Kerr, and W. A. Rogers.

Frost, himself, had detested the thought of a testimonial dinner and it was only after considerable coaxing from Charles Dana Gibson that he agreed to attend the embarrassing affair. Dana Gibson had earlier written:

> Can you let me know about when you are to get here? The boys (The Society of Illustrators) want to give you a blow out. There is no possible way of your dodging it so don't make a scene, but give in to it gracefully.

The Frosts lived comfortably in Wayne, Pennsylvania. Although Arthur, after his return from Paris, established his own studio in New York City after living with his family in Wayne for a few months, the elder Frost for the first time in years felt peacefully settled in his native land. Particularly comforting to him was the fact that the publishers continued to backlog him with illustration. He was just as busy as he had ever been. He prided himself that, as the nation's oldest illustrator, his work was still in demand, although he did admit that his eyes troubled him and that he found it necessary to spend twice the normal amount of time to get a drawing that satisfied him.

Although his older son, Arthur, was still painting pictures he did not approve of, he was very pleased with Jack's work. In spite of the fact that Jack was doing occasional illustrating on his own, the elder Frost felt that his son should acquire a little independence, so he did not interfere, although he wanted Jack to become a painter, not an illustrator. He had already interfered too much with his older son's work, Frost realized, so he'd better not meddle too much with Jack's.

Practically nothing is known about the Frost family affairs for a 12-month period following the sudden death of Arthur Frost, Jr., in 1917. There are no letters, no illustrations from this period—just a blanket of grief covers the entire year. Finally in December 1918, Daggy sent A. B. Frost the portrait that young Arthur had painted of his father in 1905, and which had been inscribed "to Uncle Gus from Arthur B. Frost, Jr."

On December 23, 1918, Frost wrote Daggy the following letter:

32 CRESCENT ROAD, MADISON, NEW JERSEY, Dec. 23rd

DEAR GUS:

The picture came safely last evening and I am more grateful to you than I can tell you. I know how much you valued it and what a sacrifice it was to give it up and I thank you from my heart.

It is even better than I thought it was, a fine thing for a boy of eighteen to do. Mrs. Frost is just as thankful as I.

We will have no Christmas. We could not have it without our boy.

I will write you again soon. I find it very hard to write anything and I have many kind letters to answer.

I am thankful that I can see that calm untroubled beautiful face all the time.

Thank you again old man.

Affectionately,

A. B. F.

Frost's grief over the death of his son is climaxed in the following letter to Daggy, written January 5, 1919:

DEAR GUS,

I am very glad to get your letter and to learn that you are all well and happy. You say you hope we are enjoying the Christmas holidays. They are over for us, it is the saddest time of the year for us and always will be. We have no Christmas and never will have again.

My poor boy's birthday and Christmas came close together and we made a great day of it. Jack feels as his Mother and I do about it and we pass the day as the other days. We gave Jack some money and some to the servants and that was all.

Jack is doing *very* well, he has gained a great deal of weight and looks remarkably well. Much better than he did before he was taken sick. The Doctor won't let him do much, but he works with me in my studio every morning for a while, about two hours. He has a story for Scribner's and plenty of time to do it in. I think we will go South in a few weeks and get away from the bad weather that is sure to come. So far the weather has been perfect. The three warm days last week were bad for Jack and he felt the effect, showing that he is not well yet.

Mrs. Frost and I are very well, I have no ailments and if I did not smoke I would feel quite up to the mark. I must stop for it does not suit me.

I have given up working in tone and am at work with a pen. I can't see well enough to work in tone, and can't get a suitable glass. I have just finished some golf drawings and am going to take up caricaturing with a view of getting into the syndicate job. If it goes at all it means better pay than I could get in any other way.

Caricature is with me a separate thing from my life. I can draw absurd things that amuse others but do not affect me. I am wretchedly unhappy and always will be but I can make "comic" pictures just as I always did. I know when they are funny but they do not amuse me in the least.

I have a hard time these days. I *must* be cheerful for Jack's and his Mother's sake and it is not easy. I wish with all my soul I were dead and with my boy and I must grin and chatter. It can't go on much longer. I will soon be 68 and my time will come some day.

No, we are not planning to go back to Phila. I would like to go but it is not the place for Mrs. Frost. She does not like it. We will stay where we are for another year. That is far enough ahead for us to look. I try to live from day to day, I wish I could stop thinking and be a machine.

Frost was, understandably, at the depths of despair at this time of his life. Still he had a son, Jack, who was yet to have a fine career as an artist and he still possessed his skill and technique as a master draftsman. Late in 1919, A. B. Frost painted an autumn landscape in water color as brilliantly as anything he had ever done. His pen-and-ink line-drawing illustrations for *The Epic of Golf* by Clinton Scollard, 1923, published by Houghton Mifflin Company (The Riverside Press, Cambridge) were equal to the very best efforts in his already long career and were infinitely superior to a similar set of golf illustrations he had done for a golfing fiction volume, *John Henry Smith* by F. U. Adams, published by Doubleday, Page & Co., 18 years earlier.

As a golfer on his 69th birthday Frost had joined, or maybe he founded, that generation of slow backswingers, who, always straight down the middle, seem to pulverize their opponents. Writing in *Collier's* magazine, December 13, 1919, Samuel Hopkins Adams, in his article, "A. B. Frost, an Unartistic Criticism," says:

I presented myself at the course just outside of Morristown, where Mr. Frost lives. Arriving late, I saw patiently practicing putts (and with formidable accuracy) a long, lank, casually built, casually garbed figure, giving an impression of marked physical endurance— a sort of seasoned toughness such as life in the open alone gives—surmounted by a striking head, white of hair and beard. A pair of shrewd, wide-set eyes twinkled at me, and the friendliest of smiles made me feel at home immediately. Straight forward I discovered that I knew the face. I had seen it in a score of Mr. Frost's own drawings. . . .

We played golf. My host played considerably more golf—or less golf, if estimated on the basis of strokes—than I did. He goes through the fair green with a low skimming ball of disconcerting length, and his approach shots are as straight to the pin as if they traveled an aerial groove. He makes the course, of rather more than average length in well under ninety, which, as he cheerfully remarked, is "pretty respectable going for a man within a few minutes of seventy years old."

In December 1919, the Frosts, without fuss or fanfare, and without any ceremonious goodbyes, moved lock, stock, and barrel to Pasadena, California. Their son, Jack, had never really acquired robust health since his bout with t.b. in Europe. His health had always seemed to hang in the balance between sick and well. Because of this, his doctors finally told him that he must live in the Southwest.

§39. "A New Jersey Landscape," oil on canvas (1898).

§40. "The Wood's Edge," oil on canvas (*c*. 1895). This canvas was probably a background study for a shooting picture.

§41. "Where the Brown Trout Lie," water color (*c.* 1885).

§42. "On the Brodhead," oil on canvas (1935). This painting by John
Frost appeared in the July 1935 issue of *The Sportsman* Magazine and
was the first of a set of six consecutive monthly sporting scenes by the
artist to appear that year.

Twilight in California

JOHN FROST left for California several months before his parents did, settling first in the desert country near Palm Springs, in the southern part of the state. The change in climate had an immediately beneficial effect, not only on his health, which improved rapidly, but on his painting as well. The desert lands with their wide spaces, fertile valleys, and majestic mountains made ideal subjects for landscape painting. So deeply did John feel the effects of this new change in environment that his work almost immediately acquired new dimension and substance. By the time his parents arrived, later that year, John had already completed some important desert landscape canvases, had sold a few at respectable prices and had sown the seed for a fine reputation as an artist of the southwest.

While John was in California in early 1919, his father, concerned over his son's health, wrote to him almost every day, giving him advice and counsel. Frost was also concerned that his son might resume professional illustrating, since it would interfere with his career as a fine painter. He writes:

> I think the sale of your pictures is a very good thing. It is encouraging, a man does not like to feel that he is painting all the time with no hope of selling anything. Sales are a sign of appreciation. I won't growl at you any more. You are doing just the thing I would have you do. I am so damn thankful you have cut illustration that I can't say enough about it. Don't give it another thought. You will never have time for any more illustration; it would be time taken from your painting and wasted.

In another letter he writes:

> Don't work hard when you start painting. You will have to stand and it is tiring. Just get

CHAPTER TEN

some fun out of it and the more fun you get out of it the better the work will be. Gosh, but you are fortunate in not being color blind, it worried me dreadfully when you boys were little. I was so afraid you might inherit it, but your brown eyes led me to believe they were different. A color blind artist is a monstrosity, it is tough as I know, I would like to paint now, but I can't do anything in oil without your help. I think I can do something in watercolor as it is not so positive and I can handle it easier.

Guy and Ethel (Rose) liked my drawings but I don't, finnicky and stupid, silly drawing of the trees, nothing broad anywhere, everything overdone and carried too far. Good Lord if I could see I could make better drawings today then I ever made, I feel things in a broader way —but it doesn't matter, I have *you*, you will be a very much bigger man than your Dad ever was—don't hurry—don't work for money, you will get there. *Think*, look at your work and *think*.

A. B. Frost's arrival in California, unlike his quiet, obscure unannounced departure from New Jersey, caused quite a stir in the California art circles and in the press. In an interview by the *Los Angeles Times*, June 14, 1920, Frost said:

I have no doubt that the California influence will appear in my work, though I see a good many of my old chin-bearded friends out here, too. I understand they come out from the Middle West on every train. But a man gets most of his pictures from his head, not from the people he sees. In Paris I used to pose a Frenchman as I wished him and then draw a picture everybody would recognize as a Connecticut farmer. From the model I got the pose and perhaps expression; all the rest came from memory, from pictures in my mind as distinct and easy to draw as models, real friends I have grown to love through long association. I don't make fun of my chin-bearded friends—I love them, and simply show their whims and humours. You see, I am a bit chin-bearded myself.

What brought you to California, after being so long identified with the East? asked a friend.

Why, the—oh, you can guess. Yes, the climate. It gets warm here in Pasadena, but there's not the humidity there is back East. My son, John, the painter, was pretty run down after he had the influenza, but when he came to California he grew stronger at once so Mrs. Frost and I came out, and—well, it's the most beautiful region we ever saw. And it makes me feel like working. So here we are for life.

Southern California should have a great future as an art center. It has everything Italy has in climate. One can work here in the year round and there is plenty of perfect stuff for landscape and marine artists. Back East the spring and autumn are the only seasons when one can work. This region might well become the American painters' paradise.

After a few months' stay in Palm Springs, the Frosts bought a home at 529 South Madison Avenue, Pasadena, and settled down for the rest of their years. Frost was still busy illustrating and his work was yet to appear for several more years, to within a few months of his death. In a 1920 letter to Daggy he mentions making four of the best drawings he had done in years for *Scribner's*. "Made them in crayon, at a flimsy desk in my room at the hotel. I'm wild to work again, after a long loaf I feel just like it. I'm going at it again hard as I can go."

His old friend Charles Dana Gibson had just bought *Life* magazine and was anxious

[136]

to add A. B. Frost to his list of contributing artists. So for the next few years Frost created a steady output of comic caricatures for *Life* to the delight of Gibson and the magazine's followers. Writes Gibson to Frost on October 3, 1920:

> DEAR ARTHUR:
> They have just sent me up an advanced copy of "Life" October 14th, and the best thing in it is your "On the Way to the Poles." It is you at your best, and no one else can do half as well, for you are a master, and "Life" is mighty proud to have you for a contributor. Casey says there is more to follow and if he is deceiving us we will fire him. We are out to make "Life" a great paper and you are doubly welcome at this time . . .

It was not long before John Frost met Priscilla Morgrage Geiger, a local sportswoman, and they were married on May 20, 1922. John was now concentrating heavily on his painting. He was awarded Honorable Mention at the Southwest Museum Exhibition at Los Angeles, 1921, the landscape prize in 1922, and the second and popular prizes in 1923, and the Gold Medal in 1924. He had now acquired the reputation of the finest landscape painter on the West Coast.

A. B. Frost's last published drawings, illustrating "A Bow to Progress," by Thomas Boyd, were in the October, 1927 edition of *Scribner's* magazine. In his last letter to his lifelong friend, Augustus S. Daggy, dated May 13, 1928, just five weeks before he died, Frost's handwriting is very weak and it is obvious that his strength was rapidly fading. He wrote:

> DEAR GUS:
> Thank you for your interesting letter. I couldn't answer it at once for my eyes were in bad shape.—
> Mrs. Frost is pretty well most of the time but she has had bad attacks of heart trouble which alarm us, she keeps up wonderfully and is fairly well most of the time. I am very seedy, I sleep very badly, lie awake half of the night and feel very tired and seedy all the next day.—
> I must stop. I hope you can read what I've written, it is a great effort for me to write.
> Love to the family,
> Affectionately,
A. B. F.

He died in his sleep on June 22, 1928, in his 77th year and is buried in Laurel Hill Cemetery, Philadelphia. Editors of many of the prominent newspapers from coast to coast wrote eloquent eulogies on the great artist, illustrator, and humorist. Many editors dusted off and republished parts of *Stuff & Nonsense*, *The Bull Calf*, and *Carlo*. Typical is the editorial in the *New York Evening Post*, June 26, 1928:

> A. B. FROST
> It is commonplace to say that realization of the death of a friend is difficult. Yet this is the manner in which the death of A. B. Frost the illustrator, must affect the American public which he served so long so finely and so gayly.
> To Frost came not one but two or even three of the greatest immortalities to which an illustrator can aspire. His pencil gave the visual form to characters imagined by other men

yet destined probably to live as long as America itself. Frost illustrated the works of Mark Twain and of Joel Chandler Harris. He created the physical semblance of Tom Sawyer, Huck Finn and Uncle Remus. He made them and all their friends as they appear today before our mind's eye. Without Frost we could not put these beloved friends into theatricals, we could not know them if we met them on the street.

Sir John Tenniel gave bodily form to Lewis Carroll's "Alice in Wonderland." Frederic Dorr Steele, we suppose created the appearance of that lesser but possibly immortal character, Sherlock Holmes. Other artists have had similar bits of brilliant fortune. But A. B. Frost, the dean of our illustrators, had even greater luck. Down through the ages, when he and we are dead and gone, his genius will twinkle on in Huck and Tom and Ole Br'er Rabbit. What price monuments of stone?

❊ *Epilogue* ❊

IN A LETTER to "Uncle Gus" Daggy, Jack had expressed the hope that "Mother might recover sufficiently after Dad's death to enjoy a little peace and happiness as she was really a splendid philosopher, but her heart trouble grew worse and there was no possible hope of recovery." Emily Frost died within six months after her husband's death.

Jack remained in California only long enough to close out the family affairs. The Frost family, which now included a son, John, Jr., a daughter, Priscilla, and their foster brother, William Geiger, now moved to the Philadelphia suburbs near Bryn Mawr to occupy the former estate of Moro Phillips, Jack's grandfather.

After a few years of hard work, which included manual labor in getting his new home in order, Jack strained some dormant tubercular scars in his lungs and it was necessary for him to enter a sanatorium for several months. His painting, though less frequent than he desired, had reached an area of almost complete fulfillment. One of his outstanding canvases, still in the possession of his family, is a marvelous winter landscape done on his Bryn Mawr estate.

Not wanting to ride the coat tails of his famous father's reputation, Jack needed considerable coaxing before he would undertake a sporting subject. His hunting and fishing companion Eugene V. Connett finally took him on a fly-fishing trip to the Brodhead Creek in the Poconos and pursuaded him to paint a fly-fishing picture, "On the Brodhead," and a landscape canvas of the river. About this time Jack painted a striking rail-shooting canvas, "Maryland Marsh," which he inscribed and presented to Mr. Connett, who, being founder and head of the Derrydale Press, published a limited edition of fine hand-colored prints from a plate engraved after the picture.

Gradually, John Frost acquired a reputation as a fine sporting artist independent of his father. His hunting and fishing scenes, unlike his father's, were always done in oil, in color, on canvas or a panel and have a look of modern elegance as distinguished from the quaint 19th-century appearance of his father's work. No comparison between the two is really possible; both were absolutely first rate.

John's last notable work was a series of six consecutive monthly color plates in 1935 for *The Sportsman* magazine. Made into inexpensively done, but rare and almost impossible to find, prints, they consisted of the fly-fishing picture, "On the Brodhead"; "Maryland Marsh"; a duck-hunting scene, "Maryland Mist"; an upland-hunting scene, "A Frosty Morning"; another duck scene, "The Limit Before Dark"; and a fine fox-hunting picture, "Autumn Morning." He mentions these pictures in a letter to Daggy, dated December 4, 1935:

> Have you happened to see a series of Sporting pictures which ran since the July issue in the Sportsman and end with the December number? I had planned a very different and much better set but was taken ill just at the start so they had to fill out the series as best they could from inferior stuff that I happened to have on hand and which I had no intention of using. It was rotten luck as the stuff isn't up to par.
>
> It's a great field (the Sporting field) and since Dad's work there's been very little of merit— so I'm going to keep banging away at it until I learn how.

At length, John, who had never really known robust health all throughout his life, was no longer able to conquer the tubercular germ, and he died on June 5, 1937, at the age of 47. Both of A. B. Frost's sons had had brilliant, but abbreviated careers. What might have been, had they both lived their full lives, makes extremely interesting conjecture.

Today John Frost, Jr., A. B. Frost's grandson, is now pursuing his own promising career as an artist in Southern California. John's sister Priscilla, now Mrs. J. W. Milliman, the wife of an economics professor at a prominent Midwestern university, is a housewife and mother, busily engaged in redecorating their home with treasures from the family collection.

Appendix: Books Illustrated by A. B. Frost

OUT OF THE HURLY BURLY, by Max Adeler (pseud. of Charles Heber Clarke). Philadelphia and New York, To-Day Publishing Co., 1874. Also St. Louis, George Maclean and Co., 1874. 379 text illus., by Frost, F. B. Schell, W. L. Sheppard, and E. B. Bensell.

ELBOW ROOM, by Max Adeler. Philadelphia, Stoddart, 1876. 49 illus.

ONE HUNDRED YEARS A REPUBLIC: OUR SHOW, by Daisy Shortcut and Arry O'Pagus (pseud. of D. S. Cohen and H. B. Sommer). Philadelphia, Claxton, Remsen, and Haffelfinger, 1876. Wrappers, 29 text illus. and pictorial cover.

SAMUEL J. TILDEN UNMASKED! by Benjamin E. Buckman. New York, Benjamin E. Buckman, 1876. 2 cartoons by Frost facing pp. 116 & 117.

ALMOST A MAN, by S. (Sarah) Annie Frost (Shields). New York, American Tract Society, 1877. 8 plates incl. front., illus., title.

PICTURES FROM ITALY, SKETCHES BY BOZ, AND AMERICAN NOTES, by Charles Dickens. New York, Harper, 1877. Numerous illus. by Frost and Nast.

AMERICAN NOTES AND PICTURES FROM ITALY, by Charles Dickens. London, Chapman and Hall, 1877. n.d. Wrappers. Imprint on front cover: New York, Appleton. (Household edition.) 8 text illus. and plate front. by Frost; 9 illus. by Gordon Thompson.

THE GHOST OF GREYSTONE GRANGE, by A. A. Beckett. London, Bradbury, Agney & Co., 1878. Frost illus. front., title page, and 2 text illus.

RANDOM SHOTS, by Max Adeler. Philadelphia, Stoddart, 1879. 17 full-page and numerous text illus., front., repeated on p. 30.

THE YOUNG NIMRODS IN NORTH AMERICA, by Thomas W. Knox. New York, Harper, 1881. Illus. by Frost, Abbey, Fenn, Rogers, and others.

FARM FESTIVALS, by Will Carleton. New York, Harper, 1881. Illus. by Frost, Abbey, Rogers, Thulstrup, Snyder, Nast, others; front. and 7 woodcut engravings by Frost.

THE FORTUNATE ISLAND, by Max Adeler. Boston, Lee & Shepard; New York, Charles T. Dillingham, 1882. Illus. by Frost and others; front. and 1 text drawing by Frost.

THE CHRONICLE OF THE DRUM, by William Makepeace Thackeray. New York, Scribner, 1882. Illus. by Frost, Pyle, Lungren, Birch, and others; 3 illus. by Frost.

NEW ENGLAND BYGONES, by E. H. Arr (pseud. of Mrs. Ellen Chapman Hobbs Rollins). Philadelphia, Lippincott, 1883. 80 wood engravings by Closson, French, Juengling, Wolf, and others after Pennell, Pyle, Frost, Smedley, Birch, and others; 6 illus. by Frost.

THE LADY OF THE LAKE, by Sir Walter Scott, Bart. Boston, James R. Osgood & Co., 1883. Illus. by Frost, Fenn, Schell, and others.

RHYME? AND REASON? by Lewis Carroll. London, Macmillan, 1883. 65 illus. by Frost for "Phantasmagoria"; 9 illus. by Henry Holliday for "The Hunting of the Snark."

HOT PLOWSHARES, by Albion W. Tourgee. New York, Fords, Howard and Hurlbert, 1883. 6 illus.

DIALECT TALES, by Sherwood Bonner. New York, Harper, 1883. 11 illus. by Frost; rest by others.

STUFF & NONSENSE, by A. B. Frost. New York, Scribner, 1884. London, Jack Nimmo, 1884. 92 pictorial pages with jingles by Charles Frost. Enlarged edition, 1888, has new cover, title page, and additional sketches and jingles.

A HISTORY OF THE UNITED STATES OF AMERICA, by Horace E. Scudder. Philadelphia, J. H. Butler; Boston, W. Ware and Co., (c. 1884). Illus. by Frost, Pyle, and others; 4 illus. by Frost.

CITY BALLADS, by Will Carleton. New York, Harper, 1886. Illus. by Frost, Pyle, and others; 5 illus. by Frost.

HUNTING TRIPS OF A RANCHMAN, by Theodore Roosevelt. New York, Putnam, 1885. Later published as *Hunting Adventures in the West*. Illus. by Frost, R. S. Gifford, and others; 5 illus. by Frost.

A TANGLED TALE, by Lewis Carroll. London, Macmillan, 1885. 6 illus. by Frost.

RUDDER GRANGE, by Frank R. Stockton. New York, Scribner, 1885. Also London, Cassell, 1885. First illus. edition. 52 illus. in *Scribner's Monthly:* "Rudder Grange," Nov., 1884; "Girl at Rudder Grange," Feb., 1878; "New Girl at Rudder Grange," Feb., 1878; "Camping Out at Rudder Grange," May, 1878; "Pomona Takes the Helm at Rudder Grange," July, 1877; "Pomona's Bridal Trip," March, 1879.

A BOOK OF THE TILE CLUB. Boston and New York, Houghton Mifflin, 1886. Illus. by club members, Strahan, F. Hopkinson Smith, Chase, Vedder, Dielman, Millet, Maynard, Quartley, Gifford, Abbey, Reinhart, Sarony, Weir, Parsons, St. Gaudens, Frost; 12 pen-&-ink line drawings by Frost.

SUCCESS WITH SMALL FRUITS, by Edward P. Roe. New York, Dodd, Mead, 1886. Illus. by Frost, Homer, Blum, W. H. Gibson, A. Kappes, and others; 1 illus. by Frost.

SEVEN AGES OF MAN, from Shakespeare's *As You Like It*. Philadelphia, Lippincott, 1885. Illus. by Frost, Church, Smedley, and others.

THE STORY OF A NEW YORK HOUSE, by H. C. Bunner. New York, Scribner, 1887. 24 halftone and line illus. by Frost. In *Scribner's* magazine, Jan.–June 1887.

FREE JOE AND OTHER GEORGIAN SKETCHES, by Joel Chandler Harris. New York, Collier, 1887. Front. by Frost.

MR. ABSALOM BILLINGSLEA AND OTHER GEORGIA FOLK, by Richard M. Johnston. New York, Harper, 1888. Illus. by Frost and Kemble; frontis. and 7 text line drawings by Frost.

VIRGINIA OF VIRGINIA, by Amelie Rives. New York, Harper, 1888. Illus. by Frost and others.

SAID IN FUN, by Philip H. Welch. New York, Scribner, 1889. Illus. by Frost, Opper, Kemble and others; 2 illus. by Frost.

OGEECHEE CROSS-FIRINGS, by Richard Malcolm Johnson. New York, Harper, 1889. 9 plates by Frost.

EXPIATION, by Octave Thanet (pseud. of Alice French). New York, Scribner, 1890. 10 plates and 8 text illus. In *Scribner's* magazine, Jan.–April 1890.

SEVEN DREAMERS, by Annie Trumbull Slosson. New York, Harper, 1891. Front. by Frost.

THE SQUIRREL INN, by Frank Stockton. New York, Century, 1891. 20 text and 13 full-page line illus. includ. front. In *Century* magazine, May–Sept., 1891.

FARMING, by Richard Kendall Munkittrick. New York, Harper, 1891. 146 text line illust. incl. title. In *Harper's Weekly*, June 7, 1890, supplement; Sept. 6, 1890–Jan. 17, 1891.

THE BULL CALF AND OTHER TALES, by A. B. Frost. New York, Scribner, 1892. Re-issued 1924, substituting "Style" for "The Kidnapping of Private Jan Francois" and "Lucinda's Stocking" substituted for "A Tale of Two Tails."

UNCLE REMUS AND HIS FRIENDS, by Joel Chandler Harris. Boston, Houghton Mifflin, 1892. 12 halftone and line plates.

THE GREAT STREETS OF THE WORLD, by Richard Harding Davis and others. New York, Scribner, 1892; also London, Osgood, McIlvaine, 1892. Illust. by Frost and others; 16 illus. by Frost.

AMERICAN ILLUSTRATORS, by F. Hopkinson Smith. New York, Scribner, 1892. Illus. by Abbey, Reinhart, Frost, Pyle, Remington, Smedley, Gibson, Church, Homer, Low, Blum, Cox, Metcalf, Zogbaum, and Kingsley; 1 full-page plate plus 4 illus. by Frost.

THE WILDERNESS HUNTER, by Theodore Roosevelt. New York, Putnam, (*c.* 1893). Illus. by Frost, Remington, and others; 2 illus. by Frost.

STORIES OF THE RAILWAY, stories from *Scribner's* by various authors. New York, Scribner, 1893. Illus. Frost and others.

STORIES OF A WESTERN TOWN, by Octave Thanet. New York, Scribner, 1893. 31 illus. In *Scribner's* magazine, Aug. 1892–Feb. 1893.

A GOLDEN WEDDING, by Ruth McEnery Stuart. New York, Harper, 1893. 6 plates by Frost, 2 by C. S. Reinhart.

THE WATER GHOST AND OTHERS, by John Kendrick Bangs. New York, Harper, 1894. 31 illus. incl. front. In *Harper's Weekly*: "The Spectre Cook of Bangletop," Dec. 9, 1891, 13 illus.; "A Midnight Visitor," Dec. 10, 1892, 9 illus.; "The Ghost Club," March 9, 1891, 12 illus.; "The Literary Remains of Thomas Bragdon," Dec. 16, 1893, 8 illus. (7 in the book).

POMONA'S TRAVELS, by Frank R. Stockton. New York, Scribner, 1894. In *Ladies Home Journal*, Dec. 1893–Sept. 1894.

THE STORY OF A BAD BOY, by Thomas Bailey Aldrich. Boston, Houghton Mifflin, 1895. 60 illus.

UNCLE REMUS, HIS SONGS AND HIS SAYINGS, by Joel Chandler Harris, New York, Appleton, 1895. New and revised edition. 112 illus. by Frost.

SHOOTING PICTURES, by A. B. Frost with text by Charles D. Lanier. New York, Scribner, 1895–96. 12 color lithos, 12 leaves of text, each with 3 text line illus.

JERSEY STREET AND JERSEY LANE, by H. C. Bunner. New York, Scribner, 1896. Illus. by Frost and others; 15 illus. by Frost. In *Scribner's* magazine, Dec. 1894 and June 1896.

TOM SAWYER ABROAD, TOM SAWYER DETECTIVE, AND OTHER STORIES, by Mark Twain. New York, Webster, 1896. Illus. by Frost and Dan Beard. In *Harper's* magazine, Aug.–Sept. 1896.

THAT FIRST AFFAIR, by John Ames Mitchell. New York, Scribner, 1896. Illus. by Frost, Gibson, Smedley, Richards, and author; 2 line plates by Frost.

FIELD FLOWERS, Eugene Field's monument souvenir. Chicago, A. E. Swift and Co., (*c.* 1896). Illus. by Frost, Remington, Birch, Lowell, Rogers, and others. Full-page halftone by Frost.

IN OLE VIRGINIA, by Thomas Nelson Page. New York, Scribner, 1896. 24 illus. by Frost, Pyle, Reinhart, Smedley, and others.

THE MISSIONARY SHERIFF, by Octave Thanet. New York, Harper, 1897. Illus. by Frost and C. Carleton.

PASTE JEWELS, by John Kendrick Bangs. New York, Harper, 1897. Front. by Frost.

SOLOMON CROW'S CHRISTMAS POCKETS AND OTHER TALES, by Ruth McEnery Stuart. New York, Harper, 1897. Illus. by Frost and others.

ATHLETIC SPORTS, compiled by Scribner's, by various authors. New York, Scribner, 1897. Several golf illus. by Frost.

FOLLOWING THE EQUATOR, A JOURNEY AROUND THE WORLD, by Mark Twain. Hartford, American Publishing Co., 1897 (*c.* Sept. 10, 1897). Published in London, Chatto & Windus, Nov. 25, 1897, as *More Tramps Abroad*. "From India to South Africa" in *McClure's* magazine, Nov. 1897, illus. by Frost and Newell; in the book this appears on pp. 609–643, but 8 of Frost's text illus. appear on other pages. Illus. by Frost, Beard, and others.

MORIAH'S MOURNING, by Ruth McEnery Stuart. New York, Harper, 1898. Illus. by Frost, Kemble, and H. M. Wilder; front. and 2 text illus. by Frost.

PASTIME STORIES, by Thomas Nelson Page. New York, Scribner, 1898. 22 illus. by Frost, 1 by Wilder. Chapters appear in *Harper's* magazine from June 1892 through Feb. 1894.

GHOSTS I HAVE MET, by John Kendrick Bangs. New York, Harper, 1898. 5 illus. by Frost; others by Newell and Richards.

THE GOLFER'S ALPHABET, by A. B. Frost, with rhymes by W. G. Van T. Sutphen. New York and London, Harper, 1898. *Harper's* magazine, Oct. 1898.

THE HEART OF TOIL, by Octave Thanet. New York, Scribner, 1898. 24 illus. by Frost.

PICTURES FROM SCRIBNER'S, portfolio of plates selected from *Scribner's* magazine, New York, Scribner, 1898. 50 plates by Frost, Gibson, Abbey, Church, Reinhart, Pyle, and others; 11 plates by Frost.

FUR AND FEATHER TALES, by Hamblen Sears. New York and London, Harper, 1899. Illus. by Frost, Tavernier, and Jaccaci; Frost illus. 6 halftone plates for "Henry's Birds," 4 for "William's Moose," 4 for "A Little Upland Game," and 5 for "Vigdal of the Jotunheim." ("Henry's Birds" appears in *Harper's* magazine, Dec., 1896 as "Wild Ducks and Tame Decoys"; "Vigdal of the Jotenheim" appears in *Harper's* magazine, Dec. 1897 as "Reindeer of the Jutenheim"; "William's Moose" appears in *Harper's* magazine, June 1898.)

THE CHRONICLES OF AUNT MINERVY ANN, by Joel Chandler Harris. New York, Scribner, 1899. 32 plates. In *Scribner's* magazine, May–Oct. 1899.

MR. MILO BUSH AND OTHER WORTHIES, by Hayden Carruth. New York, Harper, 1899. 4 illus.

THE ASSOCIATE HERMITS, by Frank R. Stockton. New York, Scribner, 1899. 9 plates incl. front. In *Harper's Weekly*, July 2–Sept. 24, 1898.

SPORTS AND GAMES IN THE OPEN, by A. B. Frost, with introduction by Frank R. Stockton. New York and London, Harper, 1899. Portfolio of 53 plates, 56 illus.

DEVIL TALES, by Virginia Frazer Boyle. New York & London, Harper, 1900. Front. and 27 halftone text drawings by Frost.

FIRST ACROSS THE CONTINENT, by Noah Brooks. New York, Scribner, 1901. Illus. by Frost, Seton, Yohn, and old prints; 1 illus. by Frost.

THE JIMMYJOHN BOSS, AND OTHER STORIES, by Owen Wister. New York, Harper, 1900. Illus. by Frost, Remington, Rogers, and Hitchcock; 4 illus. by Frost for "Sharon's Choice."

TIOBA, by Arthur Colton. New York, Holt, 1903. Front. and 3 illus. by Frost. In *Century* magazine, Nov. 1900.

UNDERSTUDIES, by Mary E. Wilkins. New York & London, Harper, 1901. Front. by Frost, illus. by others.

A BOOK OF DRAWINGS, by A. B. Frost. New York, Collier, 1904. Intro. by Joel Chandler Harris; verses by Wallace Irwin. 40 halftone plates and numerous line vignettes.

A BOOK OF DRAWINGS, by A. B. Frost. New York, Fox Duffield. Intro. by Joel Chandler Harris; verses by Wallace Irwin. 40 halftone plates and numerous line vignettes. (Same as Collier's edition except for 4 different plates.)

BRED IN THE BONE, by Thomas Nelson Page. New York, Scribner, 1904. Illus. by F. C. Yohn, Thomas Fogarty, A. B. Frost, and others. Contains one halftone plate by Frost.

THE TAR-BABY, AND OTHER RHYMES OF UNCLE REMUS, by Joel Chandler Harris. New York, Appleton, 1904. 9 plates by Frost and Kemble.

THE SOLDIER OF THE VALLEY, by Nelson Lloyd. New York, Scribner, 1904. 34 plates, incl. front. In *Scribner's* magazine, May–Oct. 1904.

THE SECOND WOOING OF SALINA SUE, by Ruth McEnery Stuart. New York, Harper, 1905. Illus. by Frost, Kemble, Fogarty, and Carleton; 6 plates by Frost.

TOLD BY UNCLE REMUS: NEW STORIES OF THE OLD PLANTATION, by Joel Chandler Harris. New York, McClure, 1905. Plates and text illus. by Frost, Conde, and Verbeck.

BACK HOME, by Eugene Wood. New York, McClure, 1905. 8 plates incl. front., title vignette, illus. stamped cover. In *McClure's* magazine: "Old Red School House," Feb., 1905, 11 illus. (2 in book); "Sabbath School," Nov., 1903, 13 illus. (1 in book); "Swimming Hole," June, 1903, 8 halftone illus. (2 in book); "Circus Day," Sept. 1905, 13 line illus. (1 in book); "Country Fair," Oct. 1905, 13 line illus. (2 in book).

JOHN HENRY SMITH, by Frederick Upham Adams. New York, Doubleday, Page & Co., 1905. Illus. by A. B. Frost.

RED SAUNDERS' PETS AND OTHER CRITTERS, by Henry Wallace Phillips. New York, McClure, 1906. Illus. by Frost, Crawford, and others. In *McClure's* magazine: "The Pets," Jan., 1904, entitled "Red Saunders at Big Bend," 9 illus. (6 in book); "In the Absence of Rules," Aug., 1904, 16 illus. (15 in book); "Where the Horse Is Fate," July, 1904, entitled "A Knot and a Slash," 3 illus. (2 in book); "A Touch of Nature," Jan., 1905, 6 illus. (3 in book).

THE PETS, by Henry Wallace Phillips. New York, McClure, 1906. One of the stories in *Red Saunders'
Pets*, published separately. 5 illus. by Frost.

LYRICS FROM COTTON LAND, by John Charles McNeill. Charlotte, N.C., Stone & Barringer Co.,
1907. Illus. by Frost and Kemble.

THE PICKWICK PAPERS, by Charles Dickens. London, A. J. Slatter, 1908. A portfolio of twelve
original illustrations reproduced from drawings by A. B. Frost. India paper edition (limited) and
plate paper edition (limited).

THIRTY FAVORITE PAINTINGS BY LEADING AMERICAN ARTISTS. New York, Collier, 1908.
Illus. by Frost, Remington, Gibson, Christy, Parrish, Kemble, Fisher, and others; "The Conciliator"
and "The Monroe Doctrine" by Frost.

CARLO, by A. B. Frost. Garden City, Doubleday, Page & Co., 1913.

AMERICAN ART BY AMERICAN ARTISTS: ONE HUNDRED MASTERPIECES. New York,
Collier, 1914. 22 plates.

UNCLE REMUS RETURNS, by Joel Chandler Harris. Boston, Houghton Mifflin, 1918. Illus. by Conde
and Frost; 4 plates, vignette on title and many text illus. by Frost.

THE EPIC OF GOLF, by Clinton Scollard. Boston and New York, Houghton Mifflin; Cambridge,
The Riverside Press, 1923. 8 line-drawing text illus. by Frost.

THE SPICKLEFISHERMAN AND OTHERS, by Frederick White. New York, The Derrydale Press,
1928. Illus. by Frost, Oliver Kemp, and Gordon Stevenson; front. and 3 text line drawings by Frost.
Also appeared in *Scribner's* magazine, 1923–24 and *Collier's*, 1924.

THE COLLECTED VERSE OF LEWIS CARROLL. London, Macmillian, 1932. Illus. by Frost,
Tenniel, Holliday, Furness, and the author.

THE UNCLE REMUS BOOK, by Joel Chandler Harris. New York, Appleton-Century, (*c.* 1935).
Retold by M. B. Huber.

Index